JKD'S WAY OF THE BLADE

BRUCE LEE'S SECRET TO KNIFE FIGHTING

JASON KOROL

MARTIAL WAY PRESS

JKD'S WAY OF THE BLADE

Bruce Lee's Secret to Knife Fighting

For further information:
Cornerstonejkd.com
Greenvilleacademy.com

Cover design by Aaron Bouchillon

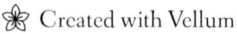 Created with Vellum

"Blessed be the peacemakers..."

INTRODUCTION

A good many people are surprised to learn that Bruce Lee had anything to contribute to the field of edged weapons. Personally, I spent 1989-1991 training with what is known as the JKD Concepts group. In particular, I was training under the guidance of renowned Dan Inosanto student, Paul Vunak. Not only that, my private Wing Chun instructor, Sifu Dan (not Mr. Inosanto, but another gentleman entirely who prefers his privacy, so I'll leave it at that), was also a Kali/Escrima practitioner. I trained privately with him from 87-92. Indeed, when it came to knife and stick, Kali and Escrima were the only game in town.

This being the case, I'd done my share of knife work from the Kali perspective during my early Jeet Kune Do years and was, in fact, teaching it. Like everyone else, I had no idea there was an alternative or that Bruce Lee himself was not particularly fond of the approach and preferred something else altogether.

Well, this leads us to the knife method I'm going to show you. I was introduced to it by Bruce Lee student Ted Wong in 1995. I'll relate the story later but for now let me just say that it was a revelation of profound importance and one I truly hope impacts you, the reader, as well. The entirety of the method is based on the same *interception concept* as Jeet Kune Do's empty hand system. In fact, they are nearly one and the same. This means that those who learn the one – JKD's empty hand method – can easily pick up JKD's knife and vice versa. Up until this point a JKD student who did Lee's original method often had to jettison the tactical/technical principles – specifically the integration of the ready-position, footwork and power side forward straight hits – in order to learn a knife method, which was usually Kali.

This, on the other hand, is something totally different. Per Bruce Lee's singular genius, it's a dynamically logical, simple and compact system. Moreover, as you'll see, it's a perfect method for the modern era of self-defense and for those civilians seeking to utilize a weapon for their protection needs. A great many knife methods taught today have a rather militaristic mindset that are difficult to integrate into civilian self-defense. We won't have that problem with this material.

Three more things before we move on.

First, please don't mistake this as an attack on either Mr. Inostanto's efforts at building weapons training into JKD or as an attack on Kali. My differentiating between them is for reasons of clarity and understanding. There are many fine Kali knife fighters out there. This is just a separate system that needs to be shared. That's all. In doing so, I'm sure there will be some who prefer the JKD method as well as those evil folks who still prefer Kali...just kidding. My case is to lay out the principles, tactics and techniques and let you draw your own conclusions from there. It's your life you're defending, after all.

Secondly, I spend a good bit of time explaining that a knife is a wonderful tool of self-defense and actually has advantages in modern life to a handgun. I do this because nearly everyone believes a gun is the *only* tool they can use for personal protection beyond their bare hands. That's just not true. So, it's in this light – the refutation of that error - that says a knife is useless in self-defense for small people, women, etc., that this material is offered. It's in no way an argument for the abandonment of firearms for personal safety. That would be epically foolish. My point is simply to expose the reader to the many advantages afforded to you by the mastery of this knife method.

And lastly, I've included a chapter on something of singular importance to everyone - the right to self-defense. I've learned a very important lesson in my life so far - if you think it goes without saying, say it anyway! It might surprise you that I'd go so far as to say that a true and logical understanding of one's right to self-defense is absolutely essential to saving and maintaining civil society. Yes, the proper understanding of one's foundational right to self-defense, and its existence as an outgrowth of political liberty, has been purposefully lost over the past few generations. That being the case, it appears to me as critical that we teach the principles of personal liberty and self-defense anew. After all, a person with a weapon in their hand for self-defense, who is ignorant of the principles that allow him/her to hold that weapon, will soon be disarmed by forces of tyranny they never knew existed.

CHAPTER 1

YOUR RIGHT TO LIBERTY & SELF-DEFENSE

SO, you have a knife. What's the goal? What are we talking about when we say, "knife fighting" or "self-defense" and things like that? Well, because of the gravity of the subject matter – and, trust me, knife work isn't something that's a game – we need to discuss a few first principles.

The first thing to be clear on is that we never, never want to kill someone. That is, unequivocally, the very worst thing that could happen, save for the loss of a loved one or ourselves. This isn't to say, however, that we consider the use of force in defense of life to be no different – or only marginally different – than the use of force by a criminal. I think we need to be as clear as possible on all of this as it's going to color everything we do in regard to the knife.

The use of self-defense by a moral person is always and forever a good thing. In defending yourself you have not "lowered yourself to their level" or some such thing. That's the kind of philosophy of cowards and moral reprobates. Even the pacifist admits there's evil and immorality in the world, they just illogically define *the use of force*, regardless of its intent, as immoral and so swear it off altogether.

This is actually evil masquerading as good; it's the proverbial wolf in sheep's clothing as far as philosophical ethics are concerned.

Let me prove it.

If you were to insist that there's no difference in the intrinsic nature of the act, then you must apply this principle to the rest of life. If violence is always bad, if the knife in the hand of the criminal is the same as that in the hand of the innocent, then you must apply this principle of reality to the whole of existence as well. In that light, there's no difference between the beauty of sex between a husband and wife on their wedding night and a rape.

I point this out because we live in morally confused/insane times. A perfect example is in those American public schools that have a policy called "no tolerance" and this no tolerance is allegedly directed to the subject of violence between students. It is, in point of fact, really a no tolerance policy toward thinking and morality because if a child is physically attacked and fights back, they get in trouble too. To think that we're raising a generation of children in public institutions where they are held captive by adults who refuse to act with moral clarity and leadership is chilling. Our kids are locked in an unethical world all day where if another child physically assaults them through no fault of their own, and they fight back, they are suspended from school. Yes, our children are reared in institutions that tell them – as a matter of open policy – that self-defense and assault are literally one and the same.

I thank God in heaven that these cowardly bureaucrats weren't in charge of America and Britain during the Second World War. And you wonder if some school administrator would think it's a good idea, an act of justice, for their wife to go to jail in the event she shot an intruder at home who was trying to rape her. That's the despicable end of the logic, after all, and we really ought to call such immorality what it is: moral hypocrisy of the highest order.

Let me be clear: the use of force in self-defense is a supremely moral action. In fact, it may very well be one of the highest moral actions available to a man or woman. This truth will likely shock those of us who have been brought up and educated in these unseemly, amoral times where good is called evil and evil good. But the attack on a sovereign individual, the initiation of force against an innocent person, is the greatest and surest violation of human rights possible. There is one great and true evil in the world in regard to relationships between people – the use of force against a free person, thereby denying their right of free will and thereby denying their humanity. This is the root of the horrible evils seen throughout history – like rape and slavery. The use of force against a person to obtain something from them they will not freely trade is always evil, and can never be, in any context, good. When the Bible says that the love of money is the root of *all kinds of evil,* it has this in mind. The love of gain without the consent of others will lead us to the initiation of force (or threat of force) against innocent people. The initiation of force (or direct threat) by a person, group, or government with the sole intent to gain a value the victim will not trade willingly, or to prohibit one's personal liberty, is the *only true violation of human rights.* All other alleged violations are a scam and ruse designed to infringe legally upon the rights of others. No human being has a *natural* right to the labors, time, property, or approval of another. When this basic and fundamental understanding of rights is understood and prac-ticed, and its violators punished through law and/or self-defense, a society is just. Notice I did not say such a society is perfect, only just. No other society can be just. No society that allows the systemic violation of consent can claim to be good.

The initiation of force, therefore, in any scenario but immediate self-defense (given the context) is evil. To disagree with this is to open the door to anarchy or totalitarianism. To disagree with this is to openly admit a preference for tyranny and the use of force against others for personal gain, whether that gain is directly material or some other value like control.

That some action or neglect of action might be wrong, or a sin, is irrelevant to this discussion. We're talking about self-defense and rights as they relate to the relationship between free people. You might be the most egregious sinner the world has ever seen, but that's none of my business. You might like to sit around all day in unwashed underpants, eating dry cereal out of a box, watching bad movies on Netflix and listening to boy-band music from the 90's. That's still none of my business. You might not like *The Outlaw Josey Wales*. Okay...wait...that's different. Off with your head!

But, seriously, it's when you physically attack me or literally restrict my actions that your sin becomes my business. All the previous is between you and God; the latter, though still a moral transgression against God, is the one that draws me into your moral orbit.

That we're teaching children in our public institutions that the use of force as self-defense is no better than the use of force for the dehumanization of others isn't simply a national tragedy. No, it's far worse than that. It's the surest sign of a moral corruption that can only be seen as a harbinger of calamity sure to come.

Think about this for a moment. The notion of self-defense – as a philosophy – rests upon the truth that all people are born free, created in God's image and, therefore, in possession of inalienable rights. This is the foundation principle behind the *Declaration of Independence*. Every word in that document rests upon the sure premise of the individual's intrinsic value and right to life, liberty and pursuit of happiness. That is, in fact, the foundation philosophy of political and individual freedom; it's the foundation for the veracity of self-defense. The *Declaration* was, after all, the world's first and only legal/philosophical document that openly declared the rights of individuals to be free from the initiation of force by their government. It identified an idea of historic importance: that every individual had a right to self-defense and just government must respect this right.

This is all so important to us – to all of us – because once we abolish the foundations upholding the truth of one's right to self-defense, we obliterate the very possibility of civil society. Once we jettison the principles of self-defense, we embrace some form of servitude and slavery. On this issue there can be absolutely no compromise any more than there can be a compromise between poison and your drinking water. To reject the premise that self-defense is *profoundly moral, loving and good* is to become a moral monster because it says that there is nothing good worth fighting for. What kind of nightmare do we create when we teach our children that there is nothing good and true and beautiful and that these are not worth vigorous defense?

Confusion on this point flows even into areas where you wouldn't think to see it. For example, in the current debate about mass-shootings and gun control in America, proponents of gun ownership often invoke their "second amendment rights." But what the government giveth, the government taketh away. The issue is freedom. Are you a free person? Or are you a slave or servant? If you are free then you have a God-given (natural right) to free speech, association, religion and so forth. The first amendment to the U.S. Constitution recognized this and declared – unequivocally – that Congress shall make no law restricting these things.

Well, the second amendment picks up where the first leaves off.

It's about recognizing the obvious. Freedom comes from God and, consequently, precedes government. A government cannot bestow freedom, only protect or abolish it.

If you're free, then you can speak your mind. You can't force people to listen to you as that would be violating their rights. You can associate with whomever you will too. But you can't force others into your group nor stop them from going to your neighbor's cookout and listening to their favorite boy-band. Freedom goes both ways. If it works for me, it works the same for you. No exceptions. If you don't have those freedoms, or if I can vote them away, then you are a servant or a slave.

And a free person has a right to defend themselves too. Period.

A slave in 1850 in South Carolina or in Rome in 70 B.C. couldn't speak their mind freely. And if their master decided to smack them around, they couldn't legally defend themselves. They were slaves. Slaves were not allowed to express themselves, go where they want, or defend themselves. This is the issue before us always – in every generation of men and women. These things don't have their genesis in race, class, sex or anything else. They're about freedom and power. And that's why it's so important that a society understand the fundamentals. Locking kids in institutions all day and telling them they can't defend themselves without getting into trouble is a way to prepare them for a life of servitude. This is partially why people talk about their "2nd Amendment rights" instead of simply declaring the moral standard of the matter: a free person can defend themselves. It isn't about hunting or fighting off criminals or a tyrannical government (although all those things are good and true) but about basic freedom.

So, why has this happened in our time? Why has the concept of self-defense been run off the road, so to speak, by our educators, media, and academics? Simply because the correct understanding of self-defense also allows one to correctly understand the nature of evil. And what is evil between human beings? Simple – it's the initiation of force, the violation of consent. Whoever refuses to honor the free will of their neighbor practices evil. And we now have a society that practices force in a variety of ways but people don't want to admit that to themselves. We don't want to admit the reality of much of what we vote for – which is the *forcing of our neighbor to do what they don't want to do merely by the power of brute, majority vote.* There is absolutely no moral right for anyone to violate the consent of his neighbor. This basic principle must be the central and guiding truth of political life of any free society. We have utterly eviscerated this foundation. Is it any wonder, therefore, why politics has become so acrimonious? It has to be in that case because neighbors are fighting over who gets the power to force each other through government.

Think about it this way. You have the moral right to put out a fire in your kitchen. A free person can certainly "delegate" that right to a fireman. Simple, right?

And you have a moral right to defend yourself against force, which can also be "delegated" to your local police.

And, naturally, you have a moral right to take money from your rich neighbor if you need it. He has too much already, so that's not fair. If your neighbor is a good fighter – and/or you're a wimpy loser afraid to risk getting clobbered – you can delegate that right to your government. Oh, wait. You have no moral right to take something from your neighbor and it's none of your business how much money he has. In that case, of course, you have no moral right to delegate to your government. This is why income and property taxation are blatant theft. They're based on the principle that your labor and your property belong to your government. The principle is so obvious that a child can follow it.

Men and women gripe incessantly that there's too much bickering in politics and how they wish we could all get along. But this is like a criminal bemoaning the fact that everyone is mean to him. When you're voting whether to steal a little more or a little less from your neighbor, you shouldn't be surprised when things get a wee bit testy.

This is why our educational institutions don't want to talk seriously about the subject of self-defense because self-defense, when properly defined, rests upon the foundation of individual liberty. We'd rather talk about minority rights and all that but, assuredly, there is no greater minority than the individual and everyone (politically speaking) has the God-given right to be left alone if he/she chooses. Instead, we live in a culture where it's taken for granted that there's some magical political right to vote for the immoral – which is, the taking of labor and property of your non-consenting neighbor. Such is a system of violence and coercion. Such is a system of theft.

So, we are left with a poisonous political culture – everyone fighting over immoral things. This is about the basic principle of self-defense, which is only true if all men and women are free. Unfortunately, our political culture sees people not as free but as groups to be used against each other in order to gain power. Is it any wonder, then, why we don't want to talk more openly about the nature of freedom and self-defense?

And, please, please, never forget this, if you can't defend yourself – if you literally cannot because you aren't allowed to – then you aren't free any more than a slave is free. You might be comfortable in your bondage, but you aren't free. You may have cool stuff, but you've sold your freedom for the newest TV and computer. You're just Neo in the *Matrix* before he took the pill.

This all needs to be said before we begin our journey on knife fighting because it's important to get the first things right. Now, when you pick up your weapon you will realize the *heart* that's behind that blade – it's a moral center that loves the good things of a good life spent and lived with honor. No other context makes sense. This isn't a game – fighting with weapons – because the questions would have to be asked. Why? Why are we fighting? What are the goals and limits?

Our answer to that is simple: our blade represents the love of our own lives, our family and our freedom. And because we love freedom we must honor it for others too. That's our ethic. The warrior shows honor because the warrior knows that a life lived without honor is a life spent in violation of the commandment to love your neighbor as yourself. To embrace the virtue of self-defense we must renounce the initiation of force both privately and publicly. That's honor. I don't want my neighbor to attack me or join a misguided and immoral collective and vote my rights away, so I will extend him the same courtesy. It's that simple. My hope is that all my readers see this and understand it. My hope is that you recognize this foundational principle and practice it. We are hypocrites of the highest order if we arm to defend ourselves but then send our government to steal from our neighbor. Honor would demand that you take your weapon and commit that act of theft yourself, citizen. If you have conjured up in your mind a right to your neighbor's stuff, go and take it by force – but do it yourself... face your neighbor fairly on a field of battle! Don't hide behind the ballot box and the guns of the government, you coward. Fight for yourself.

Are you surprised by all this? I can certainly see that you might be and understand your shock. But I have no interest in the blade – or any weapon – for the sake of it and this proves it. My interest is in the love of liberty – mine and yours. In fact, I hate weapons. But they're necessary because of evil and we need to shake this sleeping culture awake – awake to the horrors of what we're creating through our misapprehensions of what is good. There is talk of something called *social justice*. Let me be clear: it is all Marxist dogma, and Marxism is just an intellectual cover for modern slavery and mass-murder. Real social justice is freedom! Sweet and simple freedom where you may trade with your neighbor, argue with him, try and persuade him, but never use force.

Any person with a weapon who doesn't believe such is a criminal and a tyrant. Any person who doesn't swear off the violation of consent and is armed is most to be despised. Any person who doesn't, as a matter of principle, swear off the violation of consent as their guiding political ethic should face the horrific truth about their ideas. Indeed, they should admit that they want to rule over their neighbor. So, it is my good pleasure to irritate such a person. Hopefully, they change their mind when they at last see the issue clearly. If not – if they still persist in the ghastly belief that there are some exigencies that supersede freedom and that consent can be violated as a general rule of law – I don't want them anywhere near a weapon.

Of course, there are a good many who are quite simply confused by all this. They've never thought about it. And they've never thought about it because the educational system never wants them to think about it. So, we have well-meaning folks who are stuck in that dichotomy of practicing a *private* self-defense method while *publicly/politically* advocating for violence. Many people like this are sincere and truly want to help people. Ignorantly, they believe the Marxist lie that just the right amount of tyranny exercised by just the right people against some select group will perfect society. But, again, there is no such thing as a perfect society. Show me the perfect person. Show me the perfect family. Show me the perfect business. You who can't show me such small things as that are somehow duped into thinking you can have a perfect government.

No. Freedom must be the goal of politics if there is to be justice and that freedom goes to every single person without exception. (A criminal would lose his rights, of course, but a criminal would be defined only as someone who has directly violated the rights of a neighbor through force and/or fraud). Freedom doesn't care if you are black, white, gay, smart, dumb, short, tall, ugly, a good dancer or dance like Elaine Benes from *Seinfeld*. Freedom applies to everyone, and government is only there to protect every citizen's freedom and that's all. That's social justice. Justice can never mean the violation of consent against a person who is minding their own business.

I'm aware that all of this sounds to the modern ear like some kind of throwback language – and it is. But the code of honor that sees a weapon in the hands of a good guy as noble is exactly what is needed in these perilous times. The new code says that if you have a weapon with you then you must be some kind of nut. The *aggression* behind such an evaluation should be seen for what it is. The act of arming yourself for your own protection is your God-given right and duty and no one but a criminal should ever fear you – ever. To be free, truly free, is to be able to exercise the logical derivative of liberty – the right to self-defense. This modern nonsense about civilians not needing to be armed is the stuff of tyrants, spoken by people who have no problem speaking and acting freely but don't want to extend to you the same courtesy. This makes the world more dangerous, not less. Wishing that everyone would be well and peaceful is one thing – acting like the world is a safe place, free from evil, is quite another.

The reason this is a critical philosophy to understand is that a warrior's mindset, or attitude, is more important than their skill. Yes, you read that right. The wrong attitude will bleed into your situational awareness and ethical actions. If we truly understand the principle of self-defense then we'll be careful not to violate the rights of others. We won't be verbally or physically abusive to anyone. And, that being the case, we will be able to determine more clearly when our rights are being threatened. Our determination to avoid force will help us live in such a way as to be more polite and honorable to all.

Furthermore, the correct understanding of the foundation principles – that all men and women are created equal and, therefore, have *natural* political liberty given them by God, will hem in our own tendency toward narcissism and rudeness toward others. To truly treat others with respect we must know *why* that is metaphysically necessary. So, yes, I'm free. But so are you. I can trade with you, debate with you, plead with you to change your mind and so forth, but the minute I use force (or threat of force), I have violated your God-given right to liberty. It doesn't matter who you are or how loathsome I might find you. Once I initiate force (or fraud) against you, we have an issue that can only be dealt with through self-defense.

On the flip side of this is the person and society that has lost the concept of self-defense and the foundation of personal liberty upon which it rests. Such a person and society will grow more aggressive, more insulting, more tyrannical over time. Are we not seeing this happen before our very eyes? Do we not see a philosophy of anarchy and tyranny spreading in our land? The very fact that people don't speak of honor anymore is sure evidence that we don't have it. Just a generation ago it would have been inconceivable to say to another person what is routinely said on social media. Indeed, the coarsening of our culture has not politics to thank, but the individual's loss of honor – and the root of honor is the knowledge that all people are free and deserve respect.

Napoleon said that in war the moral is to the physical as three is to one. This is our point. If we live a life of honor, and know why honor is important, we won't transgress the moral line ourselves and we'll be quick to note if someone (a predator, a criminal, a politician...ah, but I repeat myself) is doing that to us. A huge point you should be careful not to miss – and the essence of everything I'm saying on this subject – is that you must decide for yourself, in your heart and soul, what you'll fight for. Fighting is about morality first, tactics and technique second and third. To miss this will leave you incapable of truly wielding the weapon of your choice. We must have the ferocity necessary to achieve the goal of protecting ourselves but this ferocity can't be simple anger, it must be indignation. It's a lot like the difference between using the *Force* or *the Dark Side.*

I have known several situations over the years where a "good" martial artist has been attacked in a school or some social setting and didn't fight back. Seriously! Let me just say, they didn't fight back because they were unclear on the moral issue of violence and self-defense. A few years ago, my son was playing a game with some other kids. One of the other children was pretty aggressive and I was keeping an eye on the proceedings (they were all about 6-7 years-old). Well, at one point, that kid got really mad at my son and really went after him. Fortunately, my son used footwork and was able to avoid the mad-rushes of the aggressor. He was taller than the other kid too, so that helped.

After the whole thing was over I asked my son about it and he said he was really surprised by the kid's rage. I told him he did a good job staying away from him but then said this: *"Listen, if that ever happens again, and you can't get away, I want you to remember this. Remember that look on his face? Remember that hatred? Good. Never forget it. And if you're faced with it and you can't escape, I want you to fight. You hear me? Use that jab and footwork, son, and punch him in the face and keep punching him until he stops. Never quit until it's over and you're safe. You understand? Match his intensity with your own, son. Never forget that."*

Well, as it went, there was another person there when I told him that and they were shocked. They indicated that what I said to "a child" was too aggressive. I told them the same thing I'm telling you. Please understand this. You must. You absolutely must. If evil and hatred attack you, you must fight and your act of fighting is a good and moral thing.

As a teacher of martial arts I see this too often. I've had people in my office tell me of their victimhood. I've had mothers weeping as they showed me video of their child being assaulted in schools while other kids cheered and filmed the assault. To not teach our children – and ourselves – of the moral nature of self-defense, therefore, is a tragic blunder.

Many instructors leave this aspect out – the moral foundation. This leads many people to wonder "what will really happen in a fight" because they sense that this all-important aspect has been neglected.

Your attitude and philosophy will dictate the way you live your life. I say all of this to make sure we all know that a person who has a weapon – any weapon – who doesn't believe in true self-defense is a horrific tragedy. On the other side, though, the moral person who is armed and prepared to defend themselves is exactly what our perishing culture needs more of, not less. Yes, an armed person, prepared for self-defense, makes the world safer, freer and more just. And an armed person, forced to fight, who knows why they are fighting, and how to fight, will have a great advantage – like three is to one – over their foe. This world needs free men and women of arms, not disarmed servants and slaves; this world needs to rediscover the foundation of self-defense, which is freedom. And this world needs to renounce – both privately and through government – the initiation of force against their neighbor who disagrees with them. This world needs to stop being told that "there is nothing you can do" in the event of a shooting or violent encounter. Yes, there is. Yes, indeed. You can fight. There is nothing wrong with losing, but everything wrong with being a coward.

Please embrace this code and this responsibility. If you say you care about others and you care about peace, then care about freedom and have your love compel you to fight when liberty is threatened. And swear to never violate the liberty of another person – either directly through your own action or indirectly through the government you support. Swear to do your part to uphold liberty because only true liberty can yield peace. True, there is "peace" under tyranny but it's the peace of slavery – the peace won through the threat of force.

What I've defined for you is sometimes referred to as the *non-aggression principle* (NAP). I have no interest in arming a person (by teaching them how to use force in the most logical manner possible) who does not uphold this principle. If, perhaps, you disagree with me I ask you to seriously and logically consider the points. The non-aggression principle is a derivative of Jesus' command to love your neighbor as yourself. My steadfastness on NAP may seem arbitrary and/or self-indulgent to you (who disagree) but please know that I am bound. There is truly no way to honestly convey this type of subject matter except on this premise. None. A true warrior seeks peace and there can be no peace so long as there is aggression (those who initiate force against others who were minding their own business). This is what I mean by being bound. The true and moral self-defender absolutely must accept the non-aggression principle or else they are a hypocrite, a narcissist and a tyrant.

The proper moral attitude will help you fight when needed. It will guide your tactics. It will alert you to danger and steer you clear from avoidable violence.

I don't offer you a knife method devoid of morality. Instead, I give you a method based upon the foundation of true morality. Nothing else is logical. Nothing else is fitting.

CHAPTER 2

THE KNIFE – SIMPLE IS BEST

I WANT you to stop for a second and imagine the type of scenario we're talking about.

First, if there is any chance at all for you to escape the encounter, do it. If you can run away, run. If you can get behind a barrier so that the bad guy can't reach you, do it. If you can hide successfully and/or stall so that help can arrive, do that too. Do not – repeat, do not – under any circumstances engage in this type of altercation without absolutely having to do so. We're talking about a life-threatening encounter. And, to be clear, the only reasons you can morally and legally use a knife in a fight is because you're in fear of imminent death, grave bodily injury, or sexual assault. A knife is rightly seen by the legal system as a deadly weapon and you can't use it except for the aforementioned reasons. Period. And the law will be rather harsh to you, as it should, if it can be determined that you *willingly* engaged in a fight – that is, you could have retreated and didn't do it. If someone called you a butter-muffin, or said you're stupid and dress funny...you can't cut them. If you're going to carry a knife with you for self-defense you must always remember to have thick skin.

Nothing should be able to draw you into a confrontation other than a direct threat to your safety. That's it.

This is the centerpiece of the intercepting philosophy of Jeet Kune Do. If you want to engage in sport based empty hand methods, that's one thing. But we cannot entertain such competitiveness here. This type of knife work is not sparring. You aren't preparing to be in a knife duel. You're preparing to utilize a blade to defend yourself against a sudden and violent assault.

With that said, we have to imagine that the stakes are high and your adrenaline is pumping. And things are going to be moving terribly fast. For this reason, you must take the emphasis on simplicity here quite seriously. Complex actions will break down under heavy stress and you'll be left with a bunch of cool moves you learned in the dojo but can't apply in a real altercation. Most knife methods – perhaps all of them by some accounts – are shot through with too much complexity. They teach multiple cutting techniques from multiple angles and all sorts of multi-movement disarms, counters and attacks. I wish I could say this more gently. I truly don't mean to sound harsh but what we're talking about is quite a serious matter. So here goes: such complexity isn't going to work and must be rejected.

Take a look at boxing, MMA and other combat sports and notice how there aren't a great variety of moves. Most martial arts have hundreds of techniques but combat sports have, for the most part, dozens – some less. Why is that? Well, under real pressure, when the other guy isn't standing still and cooperating, anything other than the most direct action won't work. This is exponentially more the case in knife work than in combat sports. JKD's way of the blade favors the simplest of actions for precisely this reason. Everything you do will be as simple and direct as possible. The thing is, though, you'll notice that it's quite difficult to remain in your discipline under pressure and that's why you must both *believe* in the veracity of this method and *practice* the heck out of it.

Literally, you're going to learn basically one move and a few variations for extreme scenarios, which, please know, are highly unlikely. Yes. I'm not kidding. There's really only the ready position, the footwork, and the basic cut. These are the heart and soul of the system and are the physical expression of what we're talking about. You aren't going to get a thousand fancy cuts. JKD's way of the blade is an integrated package-deal of the highly refined ready-position, the fencing/boxing style footwork and the basic cut. Everything else will be swirling in orbit around this integrated package.

Bruce Lee's JKD is based on Wing Chun principles and old-school boxing. When I say "old-school" boxing I mean the bare-knuckle version that emerged from fencing. This is the thing to know about JKD and our knife work. It's all based on fencing. The empty hand version of JKD can't rely on the blade so there's a little more complexity in the system – a few more strikes and more emphasis on proper body mechanics. When you have a knife in your hand, however, things become ever more focused. The blade is the key. Everything centers around that blade and you want to always stay behind it – *keep the line*, as the fencers used to say.

The small blade work here, though, is slightly different from regular fencing because you can't use a tactical folder for defense (that is, blocking) because it's too small. So, for defense, footwork becomes that much more critical than it would for the fencer. I'll say it again: the footwork is absolutely key. This truth dictates some of the differences between JKD's small blade work and fencing. But make no mistake – these principles, tactics and techniques are fencing derivatives. That is precisely where they come from, just like Lee's empty hand system.

If you like running around with your knives like kids used to run around playing cops and robbers, saying "bang", you're going to be disappointed. Sure, there are lots of things you can do with a knife and most of it really, really cool. But we've got to keep our focus on reality. Like I said, we aren't training for a demo. We aren't training to impress people. And that's what can get in the way. Our primary objective is to keep ourselves as safe as possible. For that reason, we're going to train to apply the fundamentals of the ready-position, foot-work and the basic cut. If anything violates this basic integration, we're going to reject it because it arbitrarily adds an element to our defense that exposes us to more danger than we're already in. Our rejection of other methods is based on this logic, not on subjective whim. You're going to learn to stay behind your knife (keep the line) and anything that contradicts this must logically be seen for what it is – a danger to you.

So, first, we reject complexity because it compromises our safety by damaging our ready-position/footwork/cutting mix; complexity takes our blade off-line, leaving no weapon of our own between us and danger. A good comparison is the gun. No smart shooting method teaches you to move the barrel of the gun off-target except for safety.

Secondly, we reject complexity because it often arises from our losing focus upon the primary goal, which is our safety. This sounds almost too obvious to state but, in reality, when people get a knife in their hands they often start trying to cut people. No! A thousand times no. Your goal is to defend yourself and if you have to work at getting at the guy, that likely means you could escape. Like I said, we're talking about countering an attack.

But what about all that fancy stuff we see in videos? Well, for one, it's staged.

Take a look at the demos where an instructor looks so scintillat-ing, so astonishing and check to see what the other fellow is doing. If the guy being demonstrated on is standing still – pausing – for any length of time (and I mean even a split second) you have clear evidence that what you're watching is unreal. In real life the enemy has no incentive to stand still. There's no evidence of such a thing happening consistently enough for us to depend upon it. Therefore, if you're practicing something that requires the other guy to stand still and fight a certain way, that's a good basis for discarding the method.

In real life, people move.

I can't repeat this enough, nor shout it loud enough: if you're counting on your enemy to stand still and let you do your stuff, you aren't paying attention to reality.

Simplicity is the key and by that I mean direct action supported and maintained by footwork.

The knife play you see out there generally violates this basic premise. The bad guy extends his arm or something like that and then Captain Fantastic Knife Guru Dude goes all fancy on him, cutting him so many times you half expect the man to literally fall to the floor in one-hundred bloody pieces.

And this brings us yet another problem, which is legality.

You see, in a situation like that, the death by ten thousand cuts is almost certainly going to get you incarcerated should you do that to someone. A proper knife method should always, always keep the legality of the situation in mind. As *Sifu* Tony Massengill likes to say, it doesn't do you any good to defeat one criminal and then end up in a cell with ten more like him because you used tactics that were overkill.

This issue ties directly into the previous one too. Most of the cool, fancy moves are just plain unnecessary for self-defense. The simple thing is always best. We should never forget that. If it's easy to do in training, it's going to be hard to do in a real fight; if it's hard to do in training, it will be impossible to pull off with real pressure. Of course, the issues tie together because the simplest stroke with the blade is going to cut and that cut is going to change matters right then and there, more than likely allowing you to escape, which was your goal in the first place.

The primary goal of all this is your safety, not looking cool with a blade to impress your friends. Self-defense is not hacking a guy fifty times with your war hawk. That's called murder. By keeping the main thing the main thing, we can avoid a good many errors. The self-defender doesn't want to win anything, they just want to escape and/or make the bad guy stop doing the evil and illegal thing he was doing. That's the key to the whole affair. Many mistakes are avoided when we keep this overriding principle fresh in mind. You aren't in a duel. That's a different mindset requiring different tactics and, for that matter, different weapons. A small blade isn't ideal for fighting. For that, go get a shotgun or AR-15 (which are for modern home defense and such, the premiere self-defense tools in my opinion) or at least a longer blade with a guard (to protect your precious fingers).

Why are we even having this conversation then, if the small blade is so badly suited for fighting?

Good question.

The answer is that we aren't willingly fighting with it. We are not, repeat not, in a match. I can't stress this enough. War tactics with weapons for civilians is generally called murder. Too often you see "knife training" in martial art schools and the students are sparring each other with small knives. It looks like they're trying to recreate the fight scene from *Rebel Without a Cause.* This is a lot like getting into an argument with that guy you know who's a conspiracy theorist. It's pointless. Knife sparring, for the most part, is an unrealistic exercise that will leave you exhausted but, sadly, unprepared for reality. Why the heck are you in a Zorro style blade battle anyway? What kind of life are you living that you got yourself into a small blade battle with another dude? Driving too fast and following too closely are stupid. Telling your mother-in-law that she talks too much is stupid. Many things are stupid...getting into a knife fight is downright crazy.

But the big reason is that the folding knife is the easiest self-defense weapon in the world to carry on your person. Clearly, it's not the best weapon in the world but it has the distinct advantage of being a weapon you can carry with tremendous ease. You can't carry a shotgun or AR-15 wherever you go. And in many places, you can't carry a gun – period. Readers in places that aren't America cannot legally carry a firearm, so the small blade is the logical choice.

There's a few minor points too. For example, many things in life become a mess because the people doing them aren't testing their theories with anything close to real consequences. We naturally have more respect for soldiers and firefighters than we do for politicians. This seems almost natural for us but few stop to consider the reason for it. It's an important reason and we should pay careful attention because it brings us to a central point of life under the sun. What is that exactly? It's the correct balance between theory and practice; it's epistemological in nature. Epistemology is a philosophical subject concerned with how we know what we know. It's the study of knowing. Gordon Clark said – perfectly - that all practice is the practice of some theory. That being the case, everything we do in this world is the application of a set of principles – a theory. Practice devoid of sound, logical theory is blind; theory without practice is dead.

That's the heart of the soldier/politician dichotomy. We know that a soldier is going to test his ideas against the harsh consequences of reality. If his ideas are illogical – unrealistic – then he's going to suffer. He's going to get killed. We can and should respect that. In fact, we should expect everyone to live by the same code. We should always ask – *how do you know that and where can I see this displayed in reality?* And, *can I reduce this truth back to a foundational principle without contradiction?* Such a code is uncommon, though and that's our current national tragedy. When I say that much of our life is now *political* I mean it the way a warrior means it. I mean that politicians are always forcing rules upon *others* for which they have only specious evidence and which they don't live by themselves. This is why we don't trust politicians; it's basic to the issue of trusting the correct balance between theory and practice and granting respect to those who personally test their theories. Much of the acrimony and mistrust of modern life could be swept away if only we would hold ourselves and others to this very standard. We should all *practice what we preach* (our theory). And if we can't, we should shut up. Imagine a world where we all adhered to such a code of honor as this.

Parenthetically, the best illustration of this is the so-called *stinking Amish problem.* What's the Amish problem, you ask? Well, I bet you don't agree with them about much of anything, right? I mean, you haven't eschewed modern technology and so forth and you like your life just fine. In short, you and the Amish disagree with each other on a multitude of critical points. In fact, you probably disagree far more than you agree. But, alas, you don't have a problem with them, do you? And why not? That's simple - they are living their beliefs out while leaving you alone. For that, you probably even have some respect for them although you likely believe they're being rather silly.

With this said, I will repeat my initial charge. The vast majority of knife work taught today – from the military, to the police academy, to the martial arts school, is unsuited for the realities of modern self-defense. It is often too complex and/or too aggressive to be proper for civilian use. Context is always king so we must strive to properly identify the facts of reality in order to conform to those facts. Reality doesn't care about our feelings and, as Anthony Robbins once said, no matter how enthusiastic we are, if we're running east looking for a sunset, we have a problem.

It's not my intent to imply that the men and women training and teaching some of these methods are stupid people. On the contrary, many of them are downright brilliant individuals with amazing martial art skills. The problem isn't one of intelligence or talent; it's a problem of philosophy. Philosophy is where we start – it's the big question, the foundational idea. If we get that wrong, it's awfully difficult to be right the rest of the way. So, that's the error – many of us, and I certainly did until I was corrected, think of a knife fight as either a kind of duel or some sort of special forces battle between soldiers. Both of these are grossly wrong-headed for the modern self-defender.

Consider what I'm saying this way: a sniper is indubitably a tremendous soldier – highly skilled and very dangerous – but his sniper skill set is useless in a close-range gun fight with handguns. Or: a marathoner is a superlative athlete, possessing incredible endurance, but that endurance is unneeded in a sprint. This is the point I'm making.

With this in mind, the knife work presented in this volume is brutally simple because the demands of reality are what they are and we must adapt to them, not the other way around. As you'll see, the theories are logically sound – that is, not contradictory, and the pressure testing we've subjected this methodology to has confirmed our theories. Not only that, but you will note the strong historical emphasis as well. The generations past actually fought with edged weapons because it wasn't until recently that men and women had reliable firearms. The work they did in the past informs us today, so you'll see a strong fencing influence. In fact, the fencing aspect was a key element of Bruce Lee's *Jeet Kune Do.*

There's been a common misconception in JKD over the years that Lee eschewed weapons. This isn't entirely true, but in that vacuum, Kali based blade training has been the majority report in JKD. Unknown to many, however, Lee actually investigated such methods during his lifetime and took a rather dim view of them. He preferred the much less complex methods of Western fencers to the highly elaborate Indonesian/Filipino styles. For evidence of this, take a look at the extended fight scene between Lee and his student, Dan Inosanto, in *Game of Death.* The entire scene is a dramatized, artistic elaboration of this very point. Lee used a Western timing/rhythm approach, based on footwork and simplicity, against Inosanto's more stylized and complex method. The point is even evident in the choice of clothing. Lee wore a tracksuit, symbolizing functionality and adaptation to reality; Inosanto was in a uniform, representing mindless conformity to tradition and lack of concern with reality.

This isn't meant to be critical of Mr. Inosanto's endeavors to expand the knowledge of JKD students into edged weapons and so forth. It's merely to point out the fact that Lee had seen those approaches and considered them in violation of the simplicity and directness he cherished. Nor is it an attempt to discredit those approaches either. But they are different and that must be pointed out. The JKD method of knife fighting is *fencing* based and is an extrapolation of JKD's empty hand system. Kali knife fighting has fundamental differences to the JKD style and only superficial similarities. Again – this is meant to offer intellectual clarity to the issue and not to bash the Kali methods, which certainly have their merits.

If you are in any way concerned about the veracity of my charges (if so, good for you!) don't simply take my word for it. Have a simple test. Get a dry erase marker. Take the cap off. Give it to a friend and tell him to just go for it. You probably want some goggles for safety, by the way. But have him just go after you and try to do any of the complex stuff some instructors teach. You won't be able to. Trust me. All these disarms where the instructor exhibits his extreme skill by masterfully taking a knife away from an obsequious student – they won't work. You'll never see them do one of those crazy and complex disarms against a student coming in hard with even a magic marker! Remember: if the other guy has to pause and stand still, if he has to essentially stop fighting for a second or two, it's crap. Crap. Deadly stupid crap.

Next, reverse the order. Try and go after your partner but tell them to resist. You'll notice in a hurry that complex moves still won't work even though you're fighting an unarmed guy. And if you try those complex moves, you'll probably get grabbed and end up in a bad struggle that was avoidable if you'd used more simple tactics.

The thing to remember is that you might see a knife instructor doing fancy stuff – in a demo. You won't see him/her do any of that in a live training drill, though. I've seen this myself over the years. I won't mention names so as to be respectful, but my knife instructors in more complex methods (and their top students) – when they did live drills that were unscripted – ended up doing almost the same stuff we're doing here (though not as consistently, of course, because they didn't have the proper training). Those that tried to apply the more complicated techniques failed.

This is a serious consideration. If, when faced with a dry-erase marker in the hands of a non-cooperative classmate, you can't disarm them, or defeat them with anything remotely fancy, there's no chance against a real blade that's much longer. Think about this: if a blade touches you, it's going to change your life. It isn't just an extension of someone's hand. That's foolish thinking in the extreme. A finger can't do what a knife can do. So, take a look at the size of the dry-erase marker tip and compare that to even the smallest tactical folding knife and then think deeply about this subject before moving on. The burden of proof is on the man/woman that teaches multi-movement knife work. Let them prove their theories against a dry-erase wielding combatant. And remember that the slightest mark on them represents a cut.

But for the material here you can test it and it will absolutely work under pressure testing as it correctly identifies the facts of reality and then logically prescribes the necessary training to prepare for application. It's the correct theory-practice integration. Please remember that I'm not saying this is going to be easy. Nope. I'm saying that it's going to be simple, not easy. If it's hard to do in training, it won't work under real pressure – and if it's easy to do in training, it's going to be difficult when the heat is on. Most of us get this point wrong in the safe confines of the martial art school. We do something very direct and simple and think that it was too easy, so we complicate the matter with extra movements. We must resist the temptation to do that.

The craziest thing about all this is that I found this in Bruce Lee's JKD when I wasn't even looking for it. I'll tell that story next.

A last thing to cover before we move on to that, though.

I won't be covering knife work from an offensive standpoint. This book will only cover the counter-offensive use of the blade. To do otherwise in the current day and age where terrorists and assorted madmen seek to cause mass casualties of unprepared civilians seems to me to be the height of irresponsibility – kind of like giving an alcoholic the keys to the liquor store. No. This material will only be concerned with the use of a blade for self-protection and we'll stop there. I think that's a perfectly moral standard to meet. Naturally, this will frustrate bad guys. Oh well.

I should also point out that some things have been lost in the passages of time. Some, though not all, traditional systems took a very indirect route to martial skill for the students not because they were unaware of what fighting was but because they were all too aware of what bad character was.

Think about it this way: to teach someone to use a weapon was to teach someone to kill. The masters of old took that responsibility seriously and we should too. So, many of the strange habits and training drills they had, which we scratch our heads at today and laugh, were because they were weeding out people of weak character. People who lack honor, after all, are easy to discover. Being narcissistic and impatient, they resist having to wait and suffer for anything.

Our Navy Seals and Special Forces are perfect examples of this. No one scoffs when they see a photo of these super soldiers running on the beach with a log on their collective shoulders. What does running on the beach with a log have to do with modern warfare? Well, about the same thing some of the old forms had to do with combat back then. It was all part of the training process.

That being the case, and since I can't test a reader's character that way, I'm going to refrain from including techniques and/or tactics that would assist criminals and terrorists. I could ask that you go outside and do pushups in the rain or come by my house and paint my fence but that's not too realistic. If you're so moved by the material presented here, however, and feel strongly that you'd like to do something extra for the author, please know that my wife would be quite pleased with some yard work. Just saying.

And, with all this said, perhaps one of my greatest laments against modern martial arts, besides the fact that too many instructors have messed up the theory-practice thing, is that there are too few real leaders out there. It seems that we're awash in instructors busy passing along the information of life-and-death, the keys and secrets of violence without careful deliberation about the character of those to whom they impart the knowledge. I know of several MMA schools that teach young men tremendous combat skills with nary a thought as to their responsibility for the character of those young men. Such is the tragedy of our time.

I write this book, therefore, in the spirit of love but not a love as the world now defines the word. I speak of love the way a warrior understands it. The love that compels us to self-control so that our vices never outpace our virtues and thereby hurt those we love. The love that compels honor because we don't want to contribute to a world where others are demeaned, lied to, and where disrespect is common. Honor demands that we always place doing the right thing higher than doing what we feel like doing. Honor demands that we keep our word and never ask of others what we aren't *doing* too. And a love that compels work ethic so that we can produce values to share with and serve our neighbors. And yes, a love that is aware that the good is often fragile so we're compelled to learn the martial arts in order to be prepared to defend that which is good.

In this light, no one should ever fear us unless they're evil – that is, directly transgressing the rights of others through force. A martial artist that isn't a man/woman of love is a walking contradiction at best and an ethical monster at worst. Our culture, as I said before, has turned its back on honor and character and this makes the knowledge I'm passing on more needed than in years past. This being the case, it's incumbent upon all of us to rise even higher in matters of character so as not to contribute to the moral rot that seems ubiquitous. We must resist the temptation to join the coarsening of public discourse, the horrific ad-hominem attacks, and the dehumanizing of others we disagree with, and treat all with respect right up until that moment where we must defend ourselves with force.

So, if we live lives of such honor, self-control and work-ethic, our blades will be the tools they ought to be – tools to defend that which we love.

CHAPTER 3

HOW I "DISCOVERED" JKD KNIFE FIGHTING

IT'S RATHER funny how the whole idea of JKD knife fighting was introduced to me. I'd like to report that it was because I'm a singular genius and saw through all the claptrap out there and am able to bring you the unvarnished truth. Yes, I'd like to report that. It would be a lie, though. I was just as confused as everyone else – just as given over to all the complexity – until it was explained to me.

Obviously, attaching Bruce Lee's name to something lends it some credibility but that's not the intent. It just happens to be the fact of the matter. I learned this approach directly through Ted Wong, who himself learned the principles from Lee. That being the case, it would be untruthful for me to pass this material on without proper attribution to those men. Not only that, it will hopefully give you a glimpse into the true genius of Lee's JKD principles that you hadn't previously considered even if you're a grizzled veteran of all things Bruce. Frankly, many people have no idea that Lee's thoughts on knife work were so profound – and even if they see it, the ruthless simplicity of it has a tendency to make us dismiss it out of hand. *There's got to be more to it,* we think. No, there's not. This is it.

The situation is actually quite bizarre. Whenever someone

familiar with *JKD Concepts* comes to my school and attends a knife class there's always this look of incredulity on their face as they learn the concepts and see the brilliant simplicity applied in real life. The shock is so great that I've actually been asked several times where this material came from. They're so puzzled, you see, because the brutal logic of this knife work is in direct opposition to the fancier stuff they've been taught. This is one of the great tragedies of passing off a whole system (Kali) as something it's not (JKD). Doing such a thing is intellectually dishonest on the one hand, which can be forgiven because people make mistakes, after all. But on the other hand, there's the issue that Lee's JKD principles are rather obvious to anyone who cares to look and *they certainly extend to weapons and blade work.*

Plus, there's the fact that a mistaken approach with bare fists is one thing; a structural flaw with a weapon is almost certain to be deadly. I think this just goes to show you man's natural bias against simplicity. How else can you explain the complexity-creep even amongst those that really, really ought to know better?

Well, as much as I'd like to brag and shout from the rooftops that I never made this mistake myself, I'm ashamed to relate the following story.

My great epiphany was during an impromptu training session I had with the late Ted Wong. We were standing in front of a Chinese place called, rather aptly, the Wong Restaurant. I, being rather immature and never one to pass up bad jokes, may have made a few then. Fortunately, Sifu Wong had a good sense of humor or else I never would've learned anything. Anyway, as we waited for a few other guests, we somehow got talking about edged weapons. Perhaps we ventured onto the subject because he was sick of my jokes (*how do we know the Wong restaurant is the right one?*) and was thinking of a cover for killing me. Of course, disposing of a body on an empty stomach is tough work so that might have discouraged him.

Seriously, though, before my training with him I'd been involved with the JKD Concepts stuff – which included all that fancy Kali knife and stick work. I think I may have said something about how Bruce Lee never taught weapons, or something like that. Plus, during the day's seminar training, Sifu Wong had been going over the pillars of JKD – the ready position, the lead jab and kick, the footwork, and distance control. It all seemed so basic and a few people were grumbling about that. They expected all sorts of fancy moves and he was just going over the jab and footwork for hours. So, that's the context of what we were talking about. The next thing I know, we were squared off in the parking lot with a couple of small sticks (pretending they were knives) and he asks me, "So, what's the best way to cut me?"

I stared at him and thought.

"C'mon..." he chided, "show me...what's the best way?"

"Well," I stammered and shifted my weight uncomfortably from foot to foot.

"Haven't you been certified to teach this stuff?"

"Yeah," I replied, "but it depends...it's..."

I stopped because I knew what I was going to say next was absurd. In fact, it was utterly anti-JKD. It was like saying "it depends" when your wife or girlfriend asks if you love her (or they both ask at the same time but that's a far deadlier scenario than a knife fight). It was unthinkable. I was going to say that it was complicated.

Ah!

If you know nothing about JKD and, especially, Ted Wong, you should be aware that simplicity is the key thing. I tell a story in another book of mine, *JKD Pure & Simple*, about Sifu Wong's rather comical rebuke of my hyper-complexity during a training session. I won't repeat it here in the hope that you'll go buy the book. Trust me, it's really funny...better than my other jokes thus far.

But, anyway, complexity is the antithesis of true JKD. Remember our mantra: if it's easy to do in training, it'll be hard to apply under pressure – and if it's hard to do in training, it'll never work in a real fight. Another way to see this concept is to remember that simple doesn't mean easy. Everyone forgets this in so many areas of life. Complexity creeps in everywhere and we begin majoring in minors. Well, that might add quite a bit of unneeded stress in your personal life. You might look around and think, "why do I have so much clutter around me?" Or you might wonder if you can't simplify your schedule and so on. We're always in that fight – trying to keep things simple, and trying to stay focused on the core of the issue. With all due respect to S.E. Hinton and her book, *The Outsiders,* JKD's mantra ought to be, "stay simple, Ponyboy."

Okay, so we're standing there in the parking lot, both still wearing our training clothes from earlier, starving, and I end up getting the best edged weapon class of my lifetime – the one that led to all this.

"I really don't know," I finally admitted.

And this was the seminal moment of my JKD training, frankly. I realized then, in that darkened lot, that I knew a lot of technique, but not how to really use it. I had accumulated tons of technique (practice) but no theory. At the time, I was 26 years-old and had been doing some form of martial arts or another since I was ten. But there I stood, unable to answer a simple – and rather critical question. It was humbling to admit that I truly didn't know, but as I've grown to realize in life, it isn't ignorance that's the problem, it's *false knowledge.* I knew a lot of technique so I figured I was a good knife fighter. I knew a bunch of different grips and an assortment of disarms and flows. But when it mattered, I didn't know *what to really do.*

Well, he shook his head. There was a short pause as we looked at each other standing there. Then he smiled slightly, maybe even mischievously, and then he darted forward with his right hand (which was holding the makeshift weapon) and tapped me on the chest with it. Boom. Just like that he was in and out. He dashed in, tapped me with what would have been a blade, and returned back to a safe distance.

"You see? That's it," he said with a smile. "That's the best way to cut. It's like our straight lead punch. And where did that come from?"

"From fencing?"

"Exactly!"

Finally, I got a question right.

"And that's the whole thing," he said, "if we need to be simple in hand-to-hand fighting, how much more simple do we have to be when a knife is involved?"

He went on to tell me some revolutionary things about knife combat and how it related to JKD and how Bruce Lee saw the whole issue. The next day we looked at some of the corollaries – the footwork and tactics especially – and I had a renewed respect for the fencing connection in JKD. None of the work was complex. None of the knife work, in fact, can ever be complex for the very reason that it's a knife! Simple is always best.

This is what I want to share with you. A knife is a tremendous tool for self-defense and yet most people don't consider it as valuable as a small pocket pistol. I, for one, think a person armed with a blade who has a proper education in edged weapons, is more than prepared to meet the challenges of self-defense in the modern world. Obviously, in a war zone or something like that, you'd need an increase in fire power. Yes, you'd need a gun. But for most of us, learning how to properly deploy an edged weapon and, importantly, having one with you when you need it, is more than sufficient.

Lastly, I'd very much like to introduce to the world the fact that Bruce Lee was such a martial genius that what he had to say about subjects most of us don't give him credit for – like knife fighting – was utterly brilliant. Lee's emphasis on simplicity was rooted in the cold, hard fact that real life combat wasn't a movie, it wasn't a demo, and it wasn't for fun. Real fighting is brutal and nasty. He didn't see it as a sport. He admired boxing and loved Ali – in fact, he learned much from the great books of Peerless Jim Driscoll and that man-killer, Jack

Dempsey. But he also called boxing "over-daring" too. He knew it was a game – a violent game, but a game with rules nevertheless. He brought the same mentality to weapons.

In the movie *Enter the Dragon* his character is asked by the police to go to an outlaw island to gather evidence against a man believed to be a killer and drug-producer. "It's an island fortress, really," his character is told about the place. Lee's character asks, "Why doesn't someone pull out a gun and, bang, settle it?" The agent tells him that the bad guy, Han, had a "bad experience" with guns once and won't let them on the island. So, you see...even in the movies Lee smuggled in real-life concepts. He was ruthlessly real. He knew that in real combat, when life and death hung in the balance, weapons were in play. A real martial artist needs to know how to use weapons. Period.

So, what you'll see in the ensuing chapters is given to us by Lee's JKD principles, passed down to me from Ted Wong. But lest we forget, these principles were "re-discovered" by Lee through his vigorous research. The brilliant and esteemed JKD instructor, Chris Kent, once remarked that Lee wasn't just a great athlete and warrior, he was also a scholar. Indeed, he was and it's this quality that allowed him to *go back in time* and understand that western fencing concepts were uniquely fitted to the reality of blade fighting. Most of us think only of the eastern methods but, surprise, surprise, Lee, an Asian-American, brought western weapons knowledge back to the west. It just goes to show us that the truth is the truth and it transcends race, nationality and all that.

And one more thing while we're at it.

I didn't train with Ted Wong for very long (from 95-97 and then touched base with him intermittently thereafter) but his impact was exactly what I needed. He wasn't a gifted orator. He wasn't a man that wanted to be the lead singer or guitarist of the band; he would have been happy as a roadie (or even a bass player...but I digress). He never wanted the spotlight. What brought him out of seclusion in the late-80's was the damage being done to the JKD he'd been taught personally by Bruce Lee. Like many great men who rise up, he did so because there was no one else doing it so he answered the call.

If you're reading this and you think of public speaking as desirable as a root canal, you can imagine what Sifu Wong went through in going public. Because of his unquestionable background with Lee, no one could seriously criticize him or say he wasn't qualified. He was also a uniquely humble man who refused to directly criticize others publicly. So, he brought his message of Lee's JKD – to simply simplify – to the world that desperately needed it. In doing so, he showed the true foundational principles of the ready position, fencing/boxing style footwork, straight, non-telegraphic strikes coming from the forward side, that had been ignored and, for all intent and purposes, forgotten. The response from the rest of the complex JKD world was strange to me. They ignored him.

I was expecting a vigorous debate, a spirited clash of ideas.

There was silence.

If you're too young to remember the controversies of JKD in the 90's or, perhaps, you've simply forgotten what a riotous time it was for all involved, filled with egos and bitter arguments, it's likely that you don't understand how large Ted Wong looms over Lee's method. The silence you heard from the other side (in particular, those teaching Filipino methods under the JKD banner) was the sound of defeat. Like the contemporary news media that doesn't like to report facts contrary to their political agenda, the Concepts group basically ignored him. He was quiet and humble. He spoke almost in a whisper but the ideas shouted at you. Indeed, the small, gentle man gave us JKD again – he gave us the first principles!

If you're wondering why I pause to make such a big deal out of this, please consider the previous point. There's no practice without theory. Ted Wong rescued JKD – and our weapons training too – by bringing us the forgotten (ignored) principles that made Bruce Lee. He didn't come to elevate himself. He came to elevate you and me. That's why he was so great a man and instructor and that's why I want to honor him now. Working with him convinced me that the battle is always in the mind – the apprehension of the truth (theory) and then it extends to the technical/tactical application (practice). So, to give this short-thrift will lead invariably to complexity-creep.

Frankly, it's my firm belief that every problem in the world today exists because someone or some group has forgotten or is ignoring a foundational principle. That's one of the great things JKD has taught me and I'd really like to pass this along to you too.

When we don't train our minds to seek the most direct path, we end up adding things that are unnecessary and in violation of the basic premise of the thing we're doing. This leads to new problems and then we try and solve these new problems too, not by going back to the fundamentals, but by adding even more complexity. I'm convinced that wherever you see a problem "too complex to solve" or "too confusing" it's only because the simple truth of the issue is being ignored.

Thus, in order to properly wield your blade, you must become a philosopher of the blade. There are no techniques without theory giving them direction, so we must get the first things right.

In making you a philosopher I'll be teaching you the *way of the intercepting blade*. Yes, you'll learn Bruce Lee's JKD with a knife. This is no game. This isn't some university setting where we're navel gazing. We're talking about close-combat with an edged weapon, which is bloody, nasty business. The correct theory and practice, therefore, is intended to keep us alive.

CHAPTER 4

THE ADVANTAGES OF THE KNIFE

MANY PEOPLE CARRY A CONCEALED WEAPON. In the last decade alone there has been an unprecedented growth in the number of people in America who have obtained a concealed carry permit from their state. Some of this had to do with the presidency of Barack Obama who was telegraphing at every turn his desire to limit the individual's right to a firearm. For the entirety of Mr. Obama's tenure in office it seemed like every month there was a mass shooting, followed by a press conference where he indicated there were too many guns in America, followed by people running out and buying more guns before he banned them.

Now you may or may not have paid attention to all that. You might not even live in America. And my point isn't to get into the politics of the matter. What I want to say is that when people thought they needed a weapon to protect themselves, they naturally ran out and bought a firearm. I'm not going to say that this was right or wrong. What weapon you choose to carry for your personal protection is up to you. It's none of my business. I personally believe that everyone should have and know how to use weapons for their self-defense. But what I want to address is that the knife is hardly ever considered as effective as it is and that's unfortunate since it has several advantages over firearms for personal safety.

By All Means…Bring a Knife to a Self-defense Fight

Before we get to the advantages, we must address a massive error.

It's said with such mindless regularity that most of us accept it uncritically. You've heard it. Perhaps you've said it too. You know, *"don't bring a knife to a gunfight."* We repeat it because it sounds self-evident. The problem is that we drop the context.

It's my contention that a well-trained knife fighter is better suited to deal with modern issues of self-defense than is a person with a hand-gun. I'll explain why as we move on. But first things first. The notion that a gun is always better than a knife is erroneous and we need to get this little baby put to bed.

The error we make in regard to the comparison between a knife and gun is that we lose sight of the environment and goal of their use. Obviously, a gun has greater offensive capacity at a distance than a knife. If I can't reach you, I can't cut you. The gun, though, is dangerous from greater distances. This leads many of us to close the chapter on the subject and move on. But the added range is an offensive attribute of the gun that the self-defender has little use for in the type of violent encounters we're dealing with. In fact, the added range makes self-defense literally unnecessary!

If you remember the movie, *Kill Bill*, you recall the scene where Bill's brother is killed by the Black Mamba snake hidden away in a briefcase full of cash. In the unforgettable scene, his killer, played by Daryl Hannah with that epically cool eye-patch, reads to the soon to be dead victim her research into the Black Mamba. As Bud writhes in pain on the floor in front of her, life slipping away tortuously, she says that in the African bush it's said that both the lion and the Black

Mamba can kill you – but only with the Mamba is death certain. She then adds, ominously, that's why they call it "death incarnate."

Well, there's no doubt that the lion is deadly. But fitting a lion into a briefcase full of money would have been pretty difficult. A briefcase so big to fit a lion in would have made Bud suspicious. So, you see, context is king. The knife and the gun have their place and it's patently illogical to discount the effectiveness of a knife without considering the situation it would be deployed in.

The knife, like the Mamba, is better suited for certain environments. Of course, as an offensive weapon, the gun is superior to the knife and you wouldn't want to bring a knife to a fight where you were attacking someone who had a gun and knew how to use cover. That would be suicide, not a fight. But that's not what we're talking about here.

Consider the following advantages the knife has over the handgun for self-defense.

Ease of Carry

The growth of concealed carry in the United States has been greatly fueled by very small handguns. In the last few years arms manufacturers have raced over each other to get smaller and smaller guns on the market. This makes sense since most civilians in modern America don't wear clothing that allows them to comfortably carry larger guns. This is especially true in the South and in states like Arizona and Nevada where the average temperature rivals that of the sun. If you live in a cold weather climate like Michigan you're probably already thinking of moving someplace warmer anyway (not to mention that the taxes will probably kill you before a bad guy does). Wearing cargo shorts and a t-shirt doesn't make the best outfit for carrying a full-sized handgun.

Thus, even Glock now has a single-stack .380 on the market.

There are other guns, like the Ruger LCP, another .380, that's so small it can almost get lost at the bottom of your pocket. You could be standing at the register trying to check out and you need some extra change, reach in your pocket, fish around a little, and pull out two dimes, a dirty penny from the last century, and your Ruger. *"Ah! There it is...thought I'd lost that little fella."*

Anyway, these guns are smaller and smaller simply because *they can be comfortably* carried in everyday life. A shotgun is a far better firearm for self-defense than a Smith & Wesson *Bodyguard*. No doubt. But the shotgun doesn't fit very well in your shorts and makes sitting down a little awkward. The best weapon is the one you have with you when danger happens. You can't shoot the bad guy with a weapon you don't have. Never, never forget that.

But even the smallest handgun isn't as easily carried as your basic knife. And, importantly, the smaller the gun gets, the harder it is to control. Firing a full 9mm cartridge out of a paperweight handgun is going to have considerable kick (recoil), which is going to make it hard to keep the barrel on target, which means you could be missing a lot. That desire for smaller size, therefore, is making it so that the guns are pushing the limit of application ability. More on that later.

As we'll see, there are many perfectly capable knives that weigh less than even the smallest sub-compact pistols on the market. This helps with one's ease of carry, making it more likely that you'll have the weapon with you when you need it. Personally, I have a Glock 26 as my primary concealed handgun. There are many environments where it's just too heavy and cumbersome to have on my person, but that's never the case even with my larger knives.

This hits at the most important issue we have, after all, and that's the simple truth that the best weapon for self-defense is the one you have with you right now.

There's also the issue of the environment in which we'd be using a weapon for self-defense. Most uses of a handgun in such circumstances occur within 5-7 feet. Think about that for a second. That's not very far away. For most of us, that's a couple of arm's length away.

When you couple this with the type of small guns used today for self-protection, I think you'll begin to see that the knife is quite a valid alternative. Which brings up our next point.

Self-defense isn't needed at 30 yards

If you talk to people who shoot guns regularly, you'll invariably hear someone brag about their accuracy. This is a good thing, of course. No one wants to miss their target. The problem is that this is often a misunderstood tactical concept for self-protection.

If you train at a range to shoot something at 30, 40, 50 or even 100 yards, the question must be asked: what are you training to shoot? If you aren't a soldier or SWAT team member then you have a serious legal problem. It's a bit unlikely for you to need this skill in, say, downtown Atlanta.

"Yeah, Officer, I was getting into my car after the Braves game and I saw the guy in the Washington Nationals jersey come out of the stadium. He was obviously pretty upset about the game. I mean, his team lost 6-0, and he must have paid at least $100 bucks for his seat, not including parking, and the meal for him and his family. I mean, jeez, that's like $600 for a family of four. Anyway, he was yelling at me in the distance and I noticed his 5-year-old had one of those mini-bats with him. He might have been thinking of whacking me in the knees with that sucker. And he looked a little screwed-up, if you know what I mean. Well, I wasn't taking any chances so I popped him a couple of times."

"That's a good shot."

"Yeah...two in center mass at 100 yards. That third shot took out the old lady...sorry about that. But she was pretty old anyway."

"Yeah...good point. Taking her out will save your fellow citizens on

her health care costs. Well, good job, sir. You're obviously an excellent shot."

This, quite naturally, is absurd. What scenario can you possibly imagine, short of war, where a civilian would need to engage a threat at so great a distance? You just can't think of many. In a violent encounter at a distance of more than seven yards, the self-defender should be thinking of using evasion and/or escape. At distances greater than that, we're talking about murder, not self-defense. And that's what makes the knife so perfect for the legal and moral realities of modern self-protection. You simply aren't going to cut someone you can't reach and the only reason you can reach them is that they're an imminent threat.

We must remember that the issue we're talking about – defending yourself with a weapon – has life altering consequences one way or the other. Whether you use a gun, a knife, a club, a chair... it's going to be serious. If you fail, you could die or be seriously injured. And if you succeed, you've severely injured another human being, which is nothing short of tragic. Sure, you have a moral right to defend yourself and family. That's not ever in question – and those that do question it are probably not reading this anyway. But badly injuring someone or killing them is as far down the list of things you should like to happen that it's nearly inconceivable. Short of being stuck in an elevator with your mother-in-law, there's hardly any worse scenario for a person to encounter than a life-or-death struggle with a bad guy.

The thing that makes my Atlanta scenario so absurd is the cop's reaction. If you defend yourself with a weapon you're certainly going to have to give an account for it in all but the end of the world scenarios. If you shoot or cut someone in self-defense, you're going to be talking to a police officer.

That being the case, we must have a clear apprehension of what we're talking about when we discuss the realities of self-defense.

Escape and evasion are always primary. One of the greatest lines in movie history is by Dalton in *Roadhouse*. A nurse, played by Kelly Lynch, asks him if he's ever won a fight (after taking grim inventory of all his battle scars). He replies, "No one ever wins a fight."

Exactly.

This is the crux of the whole thing. In a true fight, not a sporting match or some brain-dead ego fight, the self-defender has absolutely nothing to gain and everything to lose. This is why evasion and escape are so critical. Once the fight has been joined, the defender has already lost a lot. A successful defense will mean, even if everything went physically well for the defender, a loss of personal peace, a loss of time (providing he/she is going to have to talk with the authorities) and perhaps worse.

There are many cases where the authorities might consider your use of force disproportionate to the threat. This isn't a problem to be taken lightly. To say, flippantly, that you'd rather be tried by 12 then carried by six is true in one context – but only an extreme one. In America where there is still, at least for the most part, reasonable rule of law, your right to self-defense is generally respected. But should you use force – in particular, deadly force – in a way that's debatable – you very well might see the inside of a jail cell. Imagine that for a second. Imagine the horror and stupidity. In claiming to defend yourself against a threat, you ruin your own life by going too far or by not having properly thought through the details. Sure, you may have put a shot on target of a bad guy, but you had a chance to retreat, didn't take it, and now you're bankrupt because of all the legal fees and/or spending some time at Club Felon.

Think your neighbors are bad now?

This is a key issue in which a knife has an advantage over a firearm in modern society. Since it's a close-range weapon only, the threat has to be right on top of you for you to deploy it. That's not to say you can't still do something stupid and get yourself thrown in jail, it's just that many of us fail to consider the real-life nature of self-protection and, therefore, train for unrealistic types of encounters.

For the average self-defender, it doesn't mean a single thing that they can't shoot accurately past a few feet. Seriously. Being accurate with a handgun at more than 5 yards is, for a civilian, a bit of overkill. What type of fight are you in? How'd you get into such a battle? A life or death struggle that involves a civilian at more than 15 feet is highly unlikely. Moreover, if that's the case, long guns work quite a bit better than handguns. Your EDC (every day carry) weapon, if it's a handgun, is probably going to be deployed at a range around six to ten feet. When we get past that range it gets a little dicey both legally and morally. I mean, you're in public, for crying out loud and escape, evasion, cover and concealment should be higher on your list than engaging the threat.

Using a knife for self-protection is woefully underrated because many of us fail to take this simple point into serious consideration.

You have more control

Another aspect of using a weapon – knife or gun - for self-defense, flowing from the last one, is the issue of lethality. We need to remember that our goal as self-defenders is never to hurt anyone and certainly not to kill them. I've heard people say that if someone broke into their house and they shot them and the bad guy was down, wounded but not dead, they'd go over and "finish the guy." What a horrible, sick thing to do! That makes you a murderer. You never want to kill anyone – you just want to make them stop doing what they have no moral right to do, which is to take away your life and health. Once the threat is stopped, our counterattack must also stop.

In my state, South Carolina, we have very strong laws protecting a homeowner's right to defend themselves, their family and their property, without fear of prosecution. There was a case a few years back where a guy was having a house party. There were a lot of people at his home and some guy he didn't know, that had come with some other guest, made a few lewd comments about a picture of the owner's teenage daughter. Well, the homeowner told the guy to get lost (understandably). The guy left but then tried to come back a little while later – this time through the back door. The homeowner intercepted him and an argument ensued. Apparently, the lewd fellow refused to leave this time, so the homeowner shot him. The guy died.

I'm not sure if those were all the facts of the story. Perhaps the intruder was threatening him in some way that wasn't released to the public. Maybe he told the homeowner that he had a weapon in his pocket and he'd kill him with it. I don't know. But going on the information we have, I truly can't see how killing the guy was morally justified. In South Carolina, it was legal. The law specifically states that the owner can defend his family, himself and property if he's threatened. I'm not saying I know the whole story but this always struck me as one of those things that was most unfortunate. In that case in particular, I didn't understand why the homeowner didn't call 911 before resorting to force. Another thing about it was, if the owner felt force was appropriate at the junction, why didn't he punch the guy instead of shooting him?

Please understand, my point isn't to try and convict the homeowner here in this book. It's simply to point out some of the issues that arise in real-life scenarios. No matter what the case now, the homeowner and his family have the not so wonderful memory of killing someone in their home. That's not an easy thing to shake off. That's a memory that's not going to dissipate easily. For example, from where I'm sitting right now, writing this, I can look and see parts of my house that bring back all sorts of glorious memories. Over there on the hardwood floor was where my son, when he was little, would play cars – zooming them back and forth and making all sorts of happy noises. Ah, the memories are so glorious and precious! I'm sure you have things like that too. That's what a home is all about. So, we want to protect our homes – both physically and spiritually. Bringing death in the door if we don't have to is a terrible idea.

At the heart of this type of case is that once you fire a round from a gun, that bullet is often lethal – not always but certainly often enough. If the object is to get the bad guy to stop, killing them works but there can be other options.

Using a blade for self-protection gives you more control over lethality than firing a handgun. As we'll cover when we get to how to cut, a slash from a blade will significantly degrade the enemy's capability but is rarely lethal. Thus, a self-defender who uses a knife has the ability to deploy their weapon with a reasonable expectation that their actions will not kill the attacker. Obviously, this is no guarantee and combat is rather unpredictable. Either way, though, there's no doubt that using a blade rather than a bullet gives the defender a greater chance of *not using lethal force while still effectively defending themselves and family*. This comes into quite a clear focus when dealing with an attacker who isn't armed, or in environments where escape requires you to fight to the exit. Imagine shooting a few rounds from your 9mm when an attacker tries to grab you in a parking garage. You fire and then run off and call police. The bad guy, shot and bleeding, runs off in the other direction and later dies.

Now imagine the same scenario but, instead of a gun, you use your blade. You quickly cut him, which allows you to disengage. He tries to pursue but then realizes he's cut and bleeding. In most cases that cut (as we'll show you) won't be something that's lethal – it was, however, just enough to make him stop. And that's the goal.

To repeat our point: once you pull the trigger and the gun goes "bang", the bullet is going to go where it goes and damage whatever it damages. The penetration ability of a bullet fired from a gun is greater than the penetration ability of a snap-cut and is, therefore, more likely to be lethal. Also, due to the nature of the weapons, one cannot target the hands and arms with a gun like they can with the knife. All shooters are taught to target the center of mass. Our knife system will teach you to target (spoiler alert!) the hands and arms of the enemy. This gives the knife for the self-defender a massive advantage over the handgun because it's most consistent with the goal of *preserving* life, not taking it.

Please understand the gravity of what I just said. If you're a gun owner and you love your guns, I understand. I love mine. They're cool. But if you shoot someone in the chest with a couple of rounds from your handgun and I cut his hand, we've both achieved our primary goal – our personal safety in the event of a sudden, violent encounter. But there's more. Your bullets, while stopping the attack, might also kill the attacker whether that was your intent or not. A man with a badly damaged hand cannot carry the fight to me, but he won't die. This point brings us back to the premise of self-defense, doesn't it? We have no right to take a life; if our defense is fatal to the attacker, it's a sad consequence of having to defend ourselves but wasn't our goal. We only have a moral right to defend ourselves with the force necessary to stop an attack. On this count, the small blade is an outstanding and non-contradictory tool.

It doesn't run out of ammo

No one was ever in an altercation and wished afterwards that they had less ammo or physical energy after it was over.

In considering a knife for your self-defense, one should understand that most small handguns on the market today have a 6 plus 1 capacity. That means, for people who aren't familiar with semi-automatics, that you can have seven shots total (six in the magazine and one in the chamber). The thing about it is that you can run through shots pretty fast when you're under stress. In the past few years there's been a push by leftist politicians to limit magazine capacity. The rallying cry is that "no one ever needs more than x shots..." We pause to note that most of the people clamoring for capacity limits have never been in live firefights, life-or-death struggles and, for the most part since they're politicians, are surrounded by bodyguards who have tons of ammo. Let that sink in for a moment. There's no greater hypocrite than the knucklehead with professional armed security telling you what you don't need for your own security. It goes back to the issue of honor.

Let's be abundantly clear: the capacity for your weapon to function with maximum efficiency so long as the threat is still in play is paramount. Nothing else matters about the weapon really. If I have a gun and it's out of ammo I have in my hands an expensive brick.

This is where a knife is – at the close ranges we're discussing – much superior to most concealed carry handguns. My Glock 26 has a 10 plus 1 capacity and that's quite a bit for a gun that size but, like I said, most small .380's and 9's on the market today, that can fit in your pocket or purse, carry six in the magazine and then you need to reload or throw it at them. The knife, on the other hand, NEVER runs out of ammo. That's a huge advantage in a violent encounter. You simply never know how much the enemy is willing and able to take so it's important to have enough to stop him.

The critical error made by leftists when they preach to people that there's no need to have more than six shots is that there's just no way of knowing how many shots you need. What if you need eight but only have seven? Then what? Trust me, a reload under combat conditions isn't easy – in fact, if the threat is right on top of you, it's virtually impossible for most people (John Wick excluded, of course). But the blade isn't burdened by magazine capacity. If it's in play, it can cut. Period.

The nonsense that you don't need that many bullets is ludicrous in the extreme as it reinforces a dangerous misconception about firearms and combat. In most movies, as soon as a bad guy gets shot, he dies. The hero always gets shot in the shoulder. The bad guy, regardless of where he's hit, goes down immediately. This is utter cow stuff. It's pure fiction. No handgun round - .45's included – is ever going to knock a guy down by its pure power. Unless the shot is placed perfectly – like the brain or the heart – the bad guy is going to keep moving. And if it hits the bad guy in the brain, by the way, he's going down because he's dead, not because the firearm had "knock-down power". No handgun has knockdown power. If it did then the shooter would get knocked down too...you know, physics and all.

This is why the *capacity* of the weapon is so important. The reality of combat is that lethality and knockdown power are not the same thing. Many people are shot several times, continue their assault, and then go die later from their wounds. This reality makes the *capacity* of the knife and your footwork absolutely essential to your survival should you be in such a violent encounter. People will not just drop dead from a bullet wound unless it hits a vital target, so you must be prepared to *fight!* And that means you must be moving and have a weapon that's still capable of causing damage without reload.

It doesn't jam

Another issue in considering the difference between a handgun and a knife is the issue of a malfunction. Since a blade is a blade – there are no moving parts and no moving parts means that there's little or no chance for a blade malfunction. The gun, though, can suffer from a significant number of technical problems. Common problems come up all the time at the range and the better handlers are skilled at fixing them on the fly. Even so, that still means a critical delay when seconds absolutely count. A mis-feed will cost even an experienced gunmen a critical second or two at a time when there's little margin for error.

This is an issue that's especially pertinent to those with extra small guns because the energy released from a shot might cause so much recoil that it compromises the shooter's grip, causing a jam. Again, I'm not saying that guns are worthless for self-defense. Please don't mistake these points as me saying that a knife is absolutely supe-rior to a gun. Obviously, it's not. If I have my druthers, I'm defending myself with a Glock 19 and a few spare mags – or my shotgun. But we're talking about the context of a sudden violent encounter in the modern world. These attacks often happen at a range and location that legally and tactically give knives an advantage over guns. Everything is always about proper context.

It's multi-directional

If you were to be grabbed, the knife is still useful since it doesn't have to have the barrel pointed at the target the way a gun does. The knife has more "flexibility" in its offensive use then the gun – especially in altercations at close range where there are multiple opponents and/or grappling involved.

No "friendly fire" accidents

I think the greatest issue involved is this one. With a knife, there's virtually no chance of you killing someone you didn't mean to, which absolutely isn't the case with a gun.

In the first Persian Gulf War, after Saddam Hussein invaded Kuwait in 1990, the United States killed almost as many of their own soldiers through so-called friendly fire as they did the enemy. That's the thing about projectiles. There's a cold, hard logic to the physics. All that acceleration of a hard object is deadly and the bullet is "stupid" in that it's going to fly wherever it was pointed when fired. It doesn't stop or change directions because you didn't mean to fire it. There are no do-overs. Once that trigger is pulled and the noise-maker goes bang, that's it.

That's why every gun owner memorizes the basics of gun safety. Assume it's loaded. Never point it at anything you don't intend to shoot. Keep your finger off the trigger until you're ready to fire. AND KNOW WHAT'S BEYOND THE TARGET.

This last point is especially pertinent for the knife fighter. There's just no way for me to stab a bad guy and a good guy in a single move unless I'm wielding a mammoth sword. We're talking about tactical folding knives and things like that for EDC. You can't comfortably carry a saber in your pocket unless you're Shaquille O'Neal.

To get at the heart of self-defense – as a martial artist – it's important that we live a life of honor, love and peace. We discipline ourselves through training and self-control not only to attain high levels of functional skill but also because we're aware of the danger our own lack of control brings to our lives. Personally, I had a pretty bad temper when I was a younger man and this caused me (not to mention those around me) some rather unneeded stress. Something could go wrong early in the day and I'd be in a bad mood for hours afterwards. Who wants to be in a car with someone yelling about how bad traffic is? Who wants to live in a house with someone who flips out when their team is losing? Who wants to live with a Cowboys fan? (Sorry...couldn't help myself.)

Over the years I've learned to control my temper. Sometimes I still grow more agitated at some things then I'd like but there's been considerable progress.

This relates to martial arts because what good is it for a person to spend hours and hours developing precision skills to defend a life that they're destroying by lack of self-control elsewhere? That's a horrendous contradiction that makes a mockery of martial art training. Jesus once asked what would it profit a man to gain the whole world but lose his eternal soul? On a lesser level, what does it profit a man or woman to achieve superlative combat efficiency but ruin their marriage and/or family through lack of self-control?

I point this out because the realities of self-defense are always far different than what the movies and, especially, the video games depict. Every year people are shot and killed (or gravely injured) by negligent firearm discharges or accidental shootings. One recent heartbreaking incident I recall happened in Virginia. A father shot his teenage daughter as she was sneaking back in the house late at night. Then, obviously panicked and gripped by an unspeakable terror, he crashed his car as he was racing her to the hospital. Whether she survived or not I never did hear (that's like our media... report on bloodshed but never follow up). I would hope she did but the horror of such an event literally boggles the mind.

He shot his own daughter.

If that thought doesn't make you shudder, you shouldn't be anywhere near weapons. In fact, if the possibility of injuring an innocent person (or yourself) doesn't scare you – and I mean really scare you – you're not morally, intellectually and emotionally fit to be training with weapons. Period.

A martial artist isn't a soldier. A soldier is told when to fight and who to fight. A martial artist is a warrior/lover. A soldier fights for governments and those governments may be evil or good. There is great honor in putting your life on the line for others. A martial artist may be a soldier, of course, but he's most certainly a lover of family, peace, goodness and truth. He's a philosopher of the fist in a manner of speaking and should never, never, in any circumstances use force that's not morally justified. A martial artist, a true one, would only fight because goodness and truth demand action. No one can tell a martial artist – the private individual – when to take action because his or her own moral compass will demand it.

So, you see, the issue of friendly fire isn't a small one. The thought of accidentally ending a life or causing great bodily harm is literally the antithesis of the martial way. This is what makes using a knife instead of a gun for civilian defense so preferable. We aren't saying that using a gun is wrong or evil, of course, but the responsibility of pulling that trigger is staggering.

Imagine that a mob overruns a highway you're traveling on and members of that mob begin to reach into vehicles and attack the occupants. This scene has actually played out in America several times in the past few years due to political and racial tensions. Politics don't matter when someone tries to drag you and your family from your vehicle and pound you into the hard pavement. Love and truth demand that you defend yourself and your loved ones.

If you fire your gun into such a mob you're likely to protect yourself. But you might also hit a non-combatant. Like we said, once that bullet goes, it's gone – it's beyond your moral leadership. It's merciless. It will strike whatever or whomever is in its path – man, woman, child, friend or foe. Do you know what's beyond that target? Let's say there are protesters moving past your vehicle and your car is blocked. Some rabidly overaggressive young person decides he doesn't like the way you look and decides to have at you. He's young and strong and he breaks your car window and starts pummeling you. If you shoot, though, there are hundreds of other peaceful protestors going by too. Are you prepared to possibly kill one of them?

A knife defense, on the other hand, obliterates this worst-case scenario and is precisely why a true self-defender and martial artist should be familiar with knife work. A bad guy reaching into your vehicle is at the mercy of a good knife fighter but it's only the bad guy that's in danger, not some clueless teenager walking by that has no idea what's going on but joined the crowd because he thought it was fun.

A good mechanic uses the right tool for the job.

A good self-defender uses the appropriate weapon.

The goal is to maintain your safety with honor and truth in love. It's never to wantonly cause damage.

It's quiet – why draw attention to yourself?

With that last scene fresh in our minds, imagine having to fight your way to safety through a rioting mob. Firing a gun is going to be very loud and it's either going to cause a stampede (something you may not want) or draw unwanted attention to you and your group by other bad guys. Now, remember, the politics of this crowd is irrelevant. As I write this there are riots in Venezuela and it seems that an individual may be in danger both from civilian rioters and police officers. Situations like this are so dynamic and fluid that we do well to remember that we may find ourselves in a situation where we aren't absolutely certain what's happening and why it's happening.

Evasion and escape are the primary goals. Always. That was the issue with the homeowner shooting his daughter by accident. He forgot (or ignored) that the prime objective of a defender is peace; he fights to live, not to kill. But instead of evading what he perceived to be a threat (it wasn't) he confronted it. A defender using a knife in such instances, however, will more than likely think of evasion and escape as first priorities and engaging a threat as last resort. A civilian has no moral or legal responsibility to engage a threat in most cases with the primary exception being that loved ones are in danger. Never forget this.

Thus, if we look back at our mob/riot problem, the knife could be used only if and when the defender was unable to successfully evade and escape the mob. This gives the advantage of keeping the main thing the main thing – get out of there! Moreover, the stealth involved helps facilitate escape. The knife is soundless in a riot. No one's going to hear it. If there are bad guy police or government riot control that are trigger happy you aren't as likely to catch their attention like you would if you were firing a gun in a crowd.

Not only that but if you were to deploy your firearm in your vehicle (against someone reaching in and assaulting you or your family) it's going to rattle the cages of everyone in the car. If you think a gun range is loud – trust me, you don't want to fire a few rounds inside your car if you don't have to. In movies, you see people firing guns in tight spaces all the time and then they whisper funny one-liners to each other. That absolutely wouldn't happen in real life. If you shoot

a bad guy through your open window and then have to give instruc-
tions to the kids in the back seat, you're going to have to shout. And
even then, they probably won't hear you. The sudden reality of
violence is bad enough but when you add the booming firearm to the
mix, it can easily overwhelm the very non-combatants you're trying to
protect, rendering them immobile from shock.

Trust me, when all heck breaks loose, there's enough noise to
rattle everyone's cage – it's a significant advantage if you can keep
your defense as quiet and off the radar as possible.

A knife is more useful than a gun

Outside of shooting bad-guys, there isn't much use for your handgun
in modern life. If you need to open a box or cut some rope or string,
you aren't likely to pull out your .45 and fire away.

"Honey...why are there bullet holes in the kid's Christmas presents?"

*"Ah...oh yeah...that. Well, the boxes arrived from UPS today and I
couldn't get em open right away."*

*"Oh. Right. You're such a MAN! (And then she kisses you
passionately!!)*

Ah, no. That's not how that works – except in some strange towns in
Texas, perhaps.

A good knife has a gazillion little uses to it depending upon what
you do for a living. We aren't suggesting that a gun is useless, but
again, a knife has some built in applications for everyday life that a
handgun doesn't. And in an event where you're in the woods for
some reason – perhaps a bad-stuff-hits-the-fan bug out, for example, a
knife is still more useful than a handgun. You can open can goods

with a knife. You can clear brush away and chop it up for fire wood. You do none of that with a 9mm. And, for the record, you probably aren't going to hunt with a handgun either. That's something for your long gun. I can't imagine going all John Wick on a deer – even if said deer happened to kill your dog and somehow steal your cool car.

It's cheaper

Lastly, a good knife can cost you around $100 and many others are cheaper than that. A decent training knife might cost half that. Of course, you can spend more but I don't think it's necessary.

A gun is another story.

A decent handgun is going to run in the neighborhood of $400. I've seen the small Ruger LCP as low as $229 and Glocks around $600. Many, like the Smith & Wesson Bodyguard, go for that $400 range. Either way, the gun is going to cost you more than a good EDC knife.

But you're not done yet. The gun is useless without those bullets, you know. I always joke that it isn't the gun that's deadly, it's the bullet. A box of ammo is going to run around $10-$20 depending upon what you're shooting at the range. That doesn't sound like much but if you go shooting (and that's a necessity if you're going to be able to use the gun for self-defense) you're going to run through some ammo. It's not uncommon for many people to run through $50 worth of ammo when they go to the range.

On top of this you'll have the range fees and/or memberships depending on where you practice your shooting skills. In most places in America you can't just go outside and shoot cans anymore. That's all going to go into the cost of the gun. Most places charge something like a $10 or $15 range fee and you might need to rent (or buy) eye and ear protection. Again, for most people this is something like another $20 just to shoot (range fee plus eyes and ears). So, you bought the gun for $400 and got a "great deal" and then you bought a few boxes of ammo for $25 and then went to the range, paid for a half hour plus the goggles and ear protection.

And we're still not done. If you want to carry the gun with you (duh!) you're going to need a holster of some sort. An easy way to shoot yourself in the leg is to just put a loaded gun in your pocket. A good holster is a must. That's another charge – and they can vary from $25 up to a hundred – and more! Some holsters are pretty pricey...rumor has it that some even make coffee in the morning for you now (as justification for costing almost as much as the gun).

Oops. And don't forget that you can't just walk out of the house with it. Nope. You're going to have to be legal. Absolutely. Remember that whole contradiction thing about not making a mess of the life you're training to defend? Well, carrying illegally is a brilliant way to complicate your life in a hurry.

"No, officer, I don't have a permit and it's none of your business."

"You're right. As a private citizen, unless you commit a crime, you should never hear from your government. Oh well...have a nice day, citizen – and thanks for setting me straight."

Yeah, right. Good luck with that.

The concealed carry courses will cost you a weekend and probably another couple of hundred bucks. Just to file the forms in my state costs $50.

Okay...quick math check. Gun - $400. Ammo - $25. One day shooting at the range - $25. Holster - $50. Concealed carry permit - $200. Total - $700.

Knife - $100. Ammo - $0. Stabbing at the range – huh? Holster – pockets you already have unless you walk around naked in which case put the book down, you pervert. Concealed carry permit – none needed (more on that later). Total - $100.

Math wasn't my favorite subject but I'm pretty sure $700 is a bit higher than $100. And, what's worse, is that after that initial $700, you still need to go out and get more stinking ammo. A good gun is like a teenage son – it keeps eating through your wallet.

The other less talked about problem of gun ownership is what I call the *Special Forces Fantasy Drain* or SFFD. SFFD happens to gun owners (almost always to men) who buy a gun and then begin to have an affair with it. Remember how much money you spent when you were courting that someone special? You could never do enough. No restaurant was too much. No view was too expensive (just throw it on the credit card). Well, that's the way some guys get with their guns.

They start with a handgun. Then they read some articles and start hanging around gun shops. Then they have a new laser. Next, it's a different grip. Soon, they send it to Agency Arms and spend another $$$$$ to have it specially outfitted like a Glock gangster.

It starts to get really bad when they buy an AR. Soon, their checking account looks like a meth addict's face and they have the best guns in the world to defend the cardboard box they're living in. A Navy Seal would be proud. The problem is – beside bankruptcy – is that the Navy Seal doesn't have to buy all his stuff - the government is paying for all his toys, training and ammo. You just can't compete with that kind of cash flow. So, unless you're actually in the special forces, don't pretend you are.

But, in all seriousness, we have to look hard at ourselves. It's customary for us to fall in love with guns and weapons (knives too!) and start spending lots of extra money on them. There's nothing wrong with that. In America, it's your God-given right to be well-armed. Personally, I really like my shotguns and may have spent a little too much on them. *But they're so awesome!!* Anyway, sorry about that...the whole point is to keep things in context. If you're huge into AR's and spend more time at the range than you do at work or home, that's your choice. We just need to remember what we're talking about and that's close-quarter self-defense in a modern context where there's relative law and order. We must be able to separate our normal and everyday self-defense needs from exceptional circumstances. That's all. I'm certainly not saying that guns are useless and you shouldn't have any.

CHAPTER 5

KNIVES FOR EVERY DAY CARRY

WHEN WE SAY that you want a knife for every day carry – EDC – it's important to remind you once again that the perfect weapon you have sitting on your dresser doesn't do you any good during the life-or-death struggle outside the gas station. Therefore, in this section we're going to focus on only those types of knives that fit the bill for the following criteria:

- They are easily carried on a daily basis in a way that's safe and accessible
- They are sharp and reliable under combat stress
- They are legal to carry

Tactical Folders

For ease of carry we mean that the knife is easily concealed, easy to get at in an emergency, and something you can have with you wherever you go (for the most part).

A tactical folder gives us more carrying options than a fixed blade because the fixed blade takes up more space. Granted, the larger the knife the greater its offensive capacity. But we're going to have to give up some capacity in order to legally carry the weapon. A folding knife gives us the best of both worlds in this regard. Also, most tactical folders come with a clip so they attach easily to a pants pocket and aren't rattling around with your loose change.

There are also keychain knives which are quite small but still useful. These literally go on your keychain which makes them pretty easy to remember unless you go someplace without your keys. I have one like this (a Cold Steel mini) and a tactical folder in my pocket too.

Beyond this there is something called a neck-knife, which you can wear like a necklace. It fits into a sheath and is easy to draw and hold, which makes this little puppy a great addition to anyone's EDC arsenal. The neck-knife is a small fixed blade, making it an exception to our general rule and that just reminds us that there are lots of different ways to carry – and lots of different knives. There's just no way to adequately cover them all. My goal is to give you a simple checklist of the primary principles your EDC knife should cover in order to be legal and combat ready. If you find something that I don't mention and you like it – great. I would expect that. The issue is to meet these critical tactical points.

We should be clear on the point that there's no such thing as the perfect weapon. Give up that notion. One of the big problems for students is often the mountains of advice they get from others. I remember one instance where a young woman I know brought up the subject of guns. Well, when she did this, there was in our company a few "gun guys." Presently, she had a .22 that she carried everywhere. The gun-guys proceeded to tell her all about the disadvantages of such a small caliber handgun and the advantages of the guns they carried. This took some wind out of her sails, as you can imagine. And that's scary because the thing people need the most in a violent encounter – besides the means to defend themselves – is the confidence to follow-through, to act.

All of a sudden, she was flooded with tons of info. All of a sudden, she'd gone from being singularly focused to being overwrought with conflicting technical information.

Later, when she was able to get a moment to herself, she quietly asked me what I thought of her options. I told her the same thing I'm telling you here. Is she able to safely carry it with her daily in a way that's instantly accessible? Is it combat-ready and reliable? Is it legal to carry?

She began to ask about everything she'd just heard. Is a .45 better? What about this and that?

It's the same thing with the knife. Too much emphasis on the "perfect" knife will detract from you having and knowing how to use a weapon. As long as it meets those three key points, and you train to utilize it, you're good to go. Everyone's going to have their favorites but there's nothing perfect here on earth so don't let that discourage you. And, remember, context is king when talking about weapons and martial arts. I don't recommend a small tactical folder (or a .22) in a horrific societal collapse scenario where you're fighting almost non-stop. If that happens, God forbid, this information is useless as it pertains to a reality you aren't living in anymore. But the same goes for a mindset, weapons and tactics that fit the societal collapse scenario but not the reality of our day. Reality is always king. It (reality) doesn't care if we aren't prepared for it - and that's why false knowledge is much more dangerous than ignorance. Ignorant people are more capable of adapting quickly than those indoctrinated into false knowledge because the latter will likely persist even as evidence mounts that they're in error. Truth is the line that separates the bold from the delusional, the courageous from the merely obstinate. A master of false knowledge is literally at odds with reality and is therefore likely to act boldly in *the wrong way*. This is why it's so important not to be a philosophical *pragmatist* – but to be a *principled pragmatist.* That is, we seek to know the principles of the thing and then act.

Keep this in mind as you make your choices. There are no ultimate weapons or weapon systems (including martial arts). Reality is ultimate. We merely want to properly identify the facts of reality as it pertains to violent encounters in today's world and then arm ourselves accordingly. If you like one thing more than another, as long as it doesn't violate a principle, and you train with it, have it with you when needed, and it's legal to carry, that's the best you can do.

Okay, back to our knives.

The tactical folding knife (or the neck-knife in a sheath) must also be safe to use and carry. Like I said, if the knife can't be carried securely it becomes a danger to you. Never carry an unfolded knife or a fixed blade without a sheath. Never. Also, an EDC knife must – absolutely must – be carried in the same safe manner at all times. This is why the clip is so important so that it's fixed to your pocket. A knife that you just leave in different pockets at different times is a problem because if you need it, you're probably going to need it quickly. There won't be time to fish around your pockets when someone is attacking you. Always have your EDC knife in the same place. That's why a neck-knife or keychain knife can be your best friend.

Generally, I prefer Cold Steel knives. They stress test the heck out of the locks on their knives. You can pull up the videos on YouTube. This is important because you don't want to be in a fight and have your knife close on your fingers. The integrity of the lock on tactical folders could be the difference between you successfully defending yourself and you cutting your own fingers off. But either way, there are many fine blades out there and the choice is yours. You're the one that has to carry it and know how to use it. That's your job alone and no knife, instructor or book is going to do that for you. Just remember the basics.

The other aspect of ease of carry is that your knife, carried in the same place, must be as easy as possible to deploy. The neck-knife is simple – you just reach under your shirt and pull. The knife disengages from the sheath with a snap and your blade is live. The Cold Steel knives I use will actually open as you pull them from your pocket if you train for it. There's an opening mechanism that will catch on your clothing as the knife is pulled that opens the blade. Just like that, the weapon is live.

Switch blades work well for that too (easy opening) but they're illegal in quite a few jurisdictions because in the past they became associated with criminality. That being the case, many knives today have the ability to open them as you pull, which makes a big difference in your response time. This process has to be practiced just like any other because if you can't get your knife in play fast enough, it's as useful as a knife you left at home.

Don't defang your snake

The danger of a knife is its sharpness. A dull knife obliterates its advantage in a fight. A good sharpening tool is relatively inexpensive, not very time consuming, and keeps your blade ready to defend your life.

Most brand-new knives will be sharp enough out of the box but will dull over time and use. A small investment in sharpening tools pays huge dividends so don't neglect this extremely important issue. A sharp knife can quickly render an assault over, whereas a not-so prime blade will render what you thought of as knife-defense into a blunt object that looks like a knife. Think of the difference between a butter-knife and a steak knife. Even a spoon can come in pretty handy if you happen to jam it in the bad-guy's face, but it's next to useless for most of the things we're going to ask it to do as we move forward. The advantage of the blade is its cutting ability. If it's dull, you don't have what you think you have. It's like having an empty gun

– it looks dangerous to the naked eye and there are uses for it as a blunt object – but its primary defensive function has been muted.

The Cold Steel knives I use arrive razor sharp out of the box. In all, with a little care you should be able to keep your knife up to this standard with minimal efforts.

Legal Carry

Perhaps the worst thing that could happen to the self-defender, besides the dreaded event of being in a violent encounter we weren't prepared for, is getting arrested for having an illegal weapon. Know the laws in your state and city regarding knives. A mistake in this area can cost you thousands of dollars in legal fees and possibly your freedom.

In my home state, South Carolina, it's currently legal to carry just about any edged weapon so long as you don't use it in the commission of a crime. Obviously, there are restrictions like going to sporting events, schools and government offices. And you definitely don't want to try and get on a plane with my Cold Steel Spartan. Other than that, though, South Carolina says that if you carry a knife, just don't use it to hold up a convenience store. South Carolina was the state that fired the first shot of the Civil War, which went on to kill 620,000 people, so they aren't very bashful down here about stuff like this.

In a state like New York, though, I don't think it's legal to leave home with nail clippers. And I've heard that in California if your wit is too sharp you can end up in jail. That rules me out, of course.

Seriously, though, the laws are maddening when it comes to carrying knives across the country. And in Europe they're generally worse. Unless you're a terrorist, I don't think you can even cut a sandwich with a sharp object in the EU. This is the major *advantage* of the gun laws over knives in the U.S. – they generally allow a person with a concealed weapon permit to carry their gun when in public (with the obvious restrictions of schools and government places, etc.) but not knives. There are groups that are trying to lobby Congress to clean this up but it's slow going because – well it's Congress we're talking about and our fine elected representatives can't make money or be guaranteed votes by cleaning up bad knife laws.

In most states, though, a blade that's under two or three inches in legal. The laws vary so badly that there's no way I can safely presume to offer any counsel here so you're going to have to do a little research. A quick Google search will pull up quite a bit for you.

The other issue to consider is whether or not your knife looks like a fighting knife or a tool. This is something to consider in that if you're stopped for some reason and a police officer asks if you're carrying a weapon your response is critical. For the small knives I suggest you carry for your EDC, you can safely answer, "no...but I have my knife." What you mean by that is that you have a tool. You use a knife for all sorts of reasons at work or home. You carry a tool. A gun doesn't open boxes. If you identify your knife as a weapon when asked it can come back to haunt you in the event that you're charged with something.

Think about how the knife you're carrying will look to a jury. If you're carrying a 6-inch war blade, that looks like Rambo made it in a cave and gleefully killed a team of terrorists with it, that's going to leave a severe impression on everyone who sees it. That's something to consider when deciding on your EDC blade. My recommendation is that it should look as innocuous as possible – no unnecessary martial flourishes to make it look impressive. The *karambit* is a popular knife right now with guys who like knives. The problem is that it looks war-like and most people on a jury would see it and assume you *wanted* to use it in self-defense. Leave that for a knife you love but leave at home.

The Mini and the Spartan. Which one looks less
aggressive?

And don't worry that your knife is too small to fight with. We'll get to that. Remember that we aren't talking about a zombie apocalypse scenario. We're talking about self-protection in a world where lawyers can cause you more damage than most bad-guys. It's incumbent upon us not to lose sight of this. Obviously, the bigger the blade, the easier it is to fight with. But we can't carry a saber or a spear. As far as tactical folders go, a small blade, combined with adequate skill, knowledge and footwork can go a very, very long way, so don't despair.

All of this subjectivity in regard to the law shouldn't discourage you – and, in fact, it actually helps if you pay attention to detail.

A woman carrying a small tactical folder is going to be deemed a threat by virtually no one. If you're a 20-year-old male and you're out at 2am drinking, however, and the police stop you, you're going to invite a higher level of skepticism. This goes back to living a life of honor and of making sure you aren't making life choices that invite violence. A dad with two kids in a minivan carrying a 3-inch tactical folder in his pocket isn't going to be seen the same as a car full of young men at midnight in a bad section of town. Common sense rules.

So, in all, I don't dare tell you what knife you should use. That's up to you. But if you find the whole process too daunting and need more guidance, I'll go out on a limb and make a few suggestions. I truly like the Cold Steel AK-47 (no, it's not the gun...it's a knife). It's a great tactical folder that will fit in your pocket. It's sharp, reliable and doesn't look like a Rambo knife.

The Cold Steel Mini, which comes with a ring to fit on your key chain, is another – and smaller option. The ring it comes with is a little flimsy, so you can discard it and just attach it directly to your key chain. Don't let the size discourage you, despite being very, very small, it's a tremendous tool. Plus, because it's so small, it won't get you into legal trouble (always abide by your local laws!!!). Those are the two I'd go with – or one or the other. It's up to you. The final one is the neck knife I mentioned. A good one is the *Minimalist*. Those are my suggestions if you really don't know which way to turn. Anyone of them will work very well. Which is best? The one you will carry all the time.

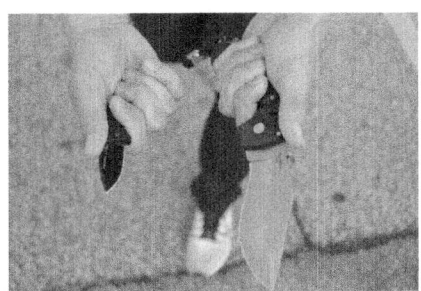

We all have our favorites, but there is no perfect
weapon

My favorite is the Cold Steel Spartan. I'm using a training version of it on the cover photo. As you can see, though, it's a pretty big, intimidating knife, so I'm careful about where I carry it. With all that said, just remember that it isn't the knife – it's you. Your training and attitude is the key. Don't worry about the perfect blade. There's no such thing.

CHAPTER 6

FIGHTING WITH YOUR KNIFE

THE ON-GUARD POSITION

First, let me say that I strongly suggest you practice the knife from both the right and left stance. Eventually. To get started, however, stand with your feet shoulder length apart (or thereabouts...you don't have to be perfect with this since everyone's built a little different) and then take a natural step forward with your preferred side. I would suggest you use your strong side since it's going to be doing all the work for you. Literally. Your rear side is meant to be kept out of the way in a knife fight.

The basic Ready-Position, which is nearly identical to
the empty hand JKD On-Guard

After you step forward I want you to pause. You'll notice when you're standing there, seemingly in limbo, that your body is telling you a few critical things.

First, your rear heel is off the floor. Leave it there. That natural step caused you to slightly push off your back foot, thus raising your heel. That's exactly as it should be. Don't drop that heel – nor should you raise it anymore either. It's likely right where it needs to be.

You'll also notice that your balance is 50-50. When you walk, you don't throw your weight forward and back. That would be quite destabilizing, not to mention exhausting. Also, you'd probably get quite a few funny looks and security would keep an extra eye on you when you're shopping if you do that. But, anyway, notice how your upper body is balanced on top of your waist, legs under you. You haven't shifted forward or leaned backward excessively unless you walk like a clown. You want your weight balanced in your on-guard stance, so get a good feel of where your weight is and make sure you aren't leaning forward one way or the other.

There's also a slight bend in your knees too. You probably never noticed this but it's all there. It's something you're already doing and we want to build on that.

Always keep the blade facing away from your body

Anyone who has ever had a child and watched them learn to walk knows that walking isn't actually natural. Falling is natural. Walking requires a series of controlled falls – just watch a child. They'll keep their knees locked, they'll step with too much momentum...all sorts of problems. So, if walking took practice, so will this. The thing is, though, once you get the hang of the on-guard and footwork, it will be just as natural to you as walking.

Next, you'll notice that you also stepped, not in a straight line necessarily, but your traveling foot made a slight curve toward the middle – your 12 o'clock. If you watch a runway model, their walk is unnatural, right? They place one foot straight in front of the other. But the other extreme is the "cowboy" – you know, someone who walks like they just got off a horse. Their stride is unnaturally wide and they step shoulder line to shoulder line. A natural step brings you toward the middle but not right at it.

Okay – get the feel of all that and now bend your knees a little more...feel the springiness of your legs and then shift slightly sideways. If you stepped forward with your right, shift to the left about 45 degrees. This will put you in a position where your toes, knees, hips and shoulders are facing *diagonally* away from the enemy. Your weight is evenly distributed. Be careful not to shift your weight forward or back in any event. Your knees are slightly bent, your rear heel is slightly elevated, and your front heel is only lightly on the floor. You want a feeling of being springy and light on your feet.

Now bring your lead arm up and place your elbow next to your hip and raise your wrist until you can point your front finger at the nose of your imaginary bad guy. Be careful not to take your elbow off your hip. Your elbow should rest (generally) to the side of the hip rather than right in front, which requires that you pull the elbow in unnaturally. This is the base position of your knife hand. As you get comfortable, move your elbow slightly off your hip (and I mean only inches) but don't let it stray too far forward. *A critical error we want to avoid is having the knife held high.* By having the knife held forward in this stance, the forearm slightly elevated from the elbow, which is backed up by the hip, your knife hand will have structural support, making it nearly impossible both to grab and overpower. If, however, you hold the knife higher, disconnected from the hip, the only thing "behind" your grip is your triceps, not your entire structure (the hip). That makes it much easier to overpower you. It also makes it easier for the bad guy to grab your arm since it's closer to him.

By keeping the blade low, the enemy can't easily grab
your wrist or arm without getting cut

You should note that the on-guard position you're in, sometimes simply called the ready-position, is ready to do two things: strike and move. Remember, the knife we're fighting with is too small to block with so our defense will be footwork. But we won't just be moving around – we'll be moving this position! Every movement we make will originate from and return to this position. The on-guard stance is, therefore, the alpha and omega of your knife fighting.

We seek to avoid a few common errors.

One, we want to avoid completely blading off the stance by putting our forward foot completely in front of our back foot. Though you would think otherwise, having a closed-stance, one shoulder forward, doesn't actually improve your reach. Once your shoulder "turns the corner" and faces away from your enemy, it breaks "the line" (the straight line between your hip, shoulder, elbow, knife and the bad guy). This actually shortens your range. Worse still, a closed-stance makes moving at angles rather difficult if not impossible. The fully squared-off stance is preferred if you are in an artificial sporting environment such as a Tae Kwon Do or fencing tournament. In those cases, they seek to limit target access by presenting as little of their body as possible. That makes sense there. But because of the rules of engagement in those environments, they have no need to move sideways very often, if at all. This isn't the case in the types of clashes we're discussing. *We absolutely must be prepared to move in a tight circle around the enemy.* Being able to move laterally or *fencing in the round* as they used to call it, makes it necessary that we're as close to being squared-off as possible without being completely squared-off. We want to "keep the line."

A longer blade than the what we're using here – like a rapier, for example – would make it less likely that you'd have to move in a tight circle because the reach of the rapier would make it quite unlikely that an enemy could get a corner on your weapon. Thus, you could close your stance off more if you had a longer blade. With tactical folders, however, we want to be mindful of the necessity to circle away from a threat.

Two, we don't want to remain opened up in our stance either. That's to say, we don't want to be squared up. We want our knife hand and hip forward. In fact, as you'll see when we discuss footwork, we will sometimes use footwork that will allow us to "hide" and momentarily blade-off while in movement so as to stay as small as possible in regard to target access of our opponent. Being squared up moves our weapon off-line (a critical, horrendous no-no) and leaves us with more target to defend – and, worse still, much of that target vital!

Do not open yourself up. By presenting only your forward side, it's much harder for you to be hit in a way that could prove deadly. This is especially pressing in the event that the enemy has a knife too.

Third, we must remember to check this on-guard position with religious fervency. You see, when you're just standing there it doesn't seem like that big of a deal. But once you start moving, firing and evading, you're going to encounter discipline lapses – you're going to shift your weight too much and all that. That being the case, don't forget to remind yourself consistently that this on-guard position is the primary thing about your knife-fighting skills. Please trust me on this, under pressure it's exceedingly hard to maintain your basics. A cavalier attitude on this point will only help facilitate a tactical/technical breakdown.

How to hold the blade

We favor the so-called thumb-reinforced saber grip. Basically, hold the knife in front of you as you would a sword and place your thumb on the back of blade. Some knives will have guards that might make the thumb placement difficult or impossible. In that event, simply grip the knife and wrap your thumb around your fingers like you're making a fist.

Simple.

The advantage this has over the other grips is that it effectively "lengthens" the blade by utilizing its full reach. Other grips, especially the "icepick" or stabbing grip, shorten the blade and brings you closer to your enemy. The stabbing, overhand grip is technically more powerful than the forward/saber grip but we really don't need to be stabbing the enemy. We're using the knife as a defensive tool. If we need to be stabbing someone (besides the obvious question of why) we should seriously consider other weapons than a small knife. Machetes, tomahawks, swords and spears are far better edged weapons than tactical folders and small fixed blades. Thus, if the zombie invasion ever does get started (probably at a Wal-Mart...that's my guess), you should use those weapons. The small blades we're talking about aren't ideal for all-out zombie warfare.

The primary function of your blade will be to snap-cut your enemy with speed. That's what we want. We want the blade to be fast and we want our attack to be voluminous. A stabbing or thrusting motion isn't ideal in that it requires more commitment and is thus slower. The forward/saber grip will give us the ability to use our knife the way Ali used his jab. That's what we want with this weapon – mobility and speed. We want to float like a butterfly and cut like a... a...well, you get the idea.

The Thumb-reinforced grip is ideal

Your stance should be knife hand forward. *Keep everything of yours behind that blade.* Don't have a single part of your body in front of that weapon. In extreme circumstances violating this rule might be necessary (we'll cover a few) but for the most part "box" or "fence" with your knife. Be light on your feet, knees bent, weight evenly distributed. The knife is too small to block or guard with so all of your defense will be with footwork and/or evasion. This is a cultivated skill that you'll only gain through hours of shadow-fighting.

The rear hand should stay back. Never let it stray forward or else it might get cut. Many bad guys use a reverse set-up. They put the knife in their rear hand and use their front to grab, shove, and post up so they can stab and thrust. The issue with this is that **they're bad guys!** The whole set-up for them is designed to kill innocent and, importantly, unarmed people. They try and sneak up on the victim, catch them unaware, grab them with the forward (free) hand and stab them multiple times. This tactic is, please know, dreadfully successful for the evil people that deploy it. But that's murder. That's not what we're up to, so this structure doesn't work for us. We want that back hand out of the way. I generally like to place mine just below my throat, on my upper chest. Others, following this logical principle, have theirs in front of their throat, covering it from a thrust (better the hand is cut than the throat, goes the thinking). There are even others that hold the free hand all the way back as if they're fencing. I don't think there's a perfect way of expressing this principled set-up so long as the principle is honored. The danger we want to avoid is having any part of our body in harm's way.

Keep your rear hand out of the way

This is the other disadvantage of holding the blade in reverse grips and so on – it places parts of your flesh in front of the blade. An icepick grip and all its variations has the blade actually facing your body. Not only does that reduce your reach, as we covered, but it also leaves you vulnerable to a cut from your own weapon should the enemy drive forward, or should you be surprised by an attack from behind. I've seen videos where a suspect is holding a knife in an over-hand grip and a police officer tackles them from behind and they end up impaling themselves as a result of the tackle. Yep, the cop gets up and the knife-holder is dead from their own weapon.

Like with the gun, don't point the knife at anything you don't intend to damage.

I'm not saying that expert knife fighters can't do such things – and do them well – but this is about the basics of self-defense, not about turning you into a super-Ninja, able to kill whole villages with a butter knife and spork.

The Snap Cut

When I said we'll be jabbing like Ali with a knife, I meant it. That's the picture you want in your mind. You're mobile, mobile, mobile. Stay behind that knife and keep your other hand out of the way! If you have any thought whatsoever of standing your ground and fighting it out, forget about it. Footwork and mobility are your new best friends.

The JKD Finger-jab and the Snap-cut follow the same principles - but the knife, of course, is far more dangerous

The thing is, though, we aren't going to be actually jabbing with the blade. The jab needs to travel in a straight line to the target in order to land properly with the knuckles. In that way, a jab is a thrust punch. The knife, however, brings an ever so slight and different dynamic to it. We don't need much power. We merely need to touch the bad guy – fast and often. To do this, we'll use a hybrid motion specific to the blade. The old fencers called this basic action the "Snap-Cut" because the wrist snapped as the arm shot forward. I have no problem with this terminology. I call it a "jab-cut" sometimes merely to reinforce in our minds the necessity of Ali jab-type attacks with the blade rather than slower thrusting attacks.

An easy way to understand the action is to grab a small hand towel, place it in your hand like it's your knife, assume your on-guard position, and then whip it – you can even hum the *Devo* song as you do it. We've all done this with towels, right? Well, it's exactly the action we want now with the blade. It's that snap at the end that we want. This is so critical to our success in applying this style that I suggest you do this with the towel first. It's so important, in fact, that you can't really do too much training like this as it will keep you focused on speed and snap. (*Remember to train slowly at first, using good form and to pace yourself. Going too fast too soon and too often could lead to an arm and/or elbow injury*).

The goal is to get your knife as fast as possible and be able to snap several shots in a quick series while moving. When you can achieve this consistently, trust me, no one will want to mess with you when you have a knife. This is all you ever truly need to do for self-defense! Everything else is quite superfluous after this point. I mean this. Seriously. This is all you ever need to do. When you can move and snap/jab, you become an extraordinarily difficult target to defeat. Everything else we will cover is simply an extrapolation of this fundamental tactic and/or a response to a difficulty in the move-and-cut style.

The Basic Snap-Cut

A huge mistake to watch for – and a reason why you absolutely must practice this! – is bringing the knife back to you after a strike. If you've boxed or done MMA – any method where keeping your hands up is drilled into you – you need to be especially vigilant against this habit. After each cut the blade should never come back near your face. The problem is that a trained boxer, for example, is an expert at snapping a jab forward and then bringing his hand back to his chin. This could be huge trouble with a knife in your hand.

"Hey, Bob...how'd you get that hole in your face?"

"The retraction of my snap-cut, dude. I rebounded off a strike and popped myself in the cheek with my own knife. The doctor says I'll be okay, though it sucks having to wear this bib all the time. Drinking through a straw is impossible now too. Oh, well."

"Well at least you beat the bad guy."

Using the blade properly will greatly increase your
reach

Train diligently to execute the basic strike in combination,
returning to the on-guard stance every time. What you'll notice is
that you have to be constantly aware of the tendency for your rear
hand to drift into play and for your knife to break the rule about
never facing your body. Train slowly to get the hang of it and pick up
speed only when your form is good. I can't repeat this often enough:
the economy of motion of this basic cut – combined later with your
footwork – will allow you to maintain an amazing rate of fire and
keep you safe from grabs. The directness of the action will make you
fast and that speed will allow you to attack in a nearly continuous
fashion.

As always, simple never means easy. It only looks easy.

Angles of the Cut

When using angles, be careful not to open up

The blade gives you a great advantage over Ali. You see, Ali couldn't just touch his opponent and hurt them. He had to deliver sufficient force through his body mechanics and that force had to be conveyed through a specific delivery position of his fist. The knife, on the other hand, merely needs to touch the target with enough speed and the sharpness of the blade will do the rest for you.

What this means is that you can change the angle of your cut slightly without losing the effectiveness of the strike.

Shifting the upper body and stepping to the angle

The thing to remember as this goes is that you can and should snap/jab-cut at any angle you need to so long as you don't start swinging the blade around. The larger the motion of your arm, the greater your risk. Keep everything as compact as possible.

The basic cut will travel straight forward and finish with a slight downward snap of the wrist and blade. This finishing action gives the blade a bit of pop and the better you are at doing this, the deeper the cut will be. Obviously, the stronger you are, and the sharper your knife is, the more damage this basic action will cause. The key is always speed. Don't try and do too much with any single action or else you can get over-extended, which can lead to your hand being grabbed and/or your position getting overrun.

More than this, though, is that you can change the angle of your hand to use the snap/jab-cut from either side and even upside down! If you were snap-cutting at a clock, your basic cut will be straight away at 12. But you can easily change the angle and snap-cut at 1, or

11, or 2 and 10 too. And, remember, you can do this in blindingly fast combinations – while on the move! Just make sure to keep the action compact. If you begin to open up your movement by bringing your arm away from the line separating you from your enemy, you're leaving yourself open. Practice diligently to be able to do this with the utmost economy of motion.

Be careful not to bring your blade off-line, thus exposing yourself to a grab or cut

A snap/jab-cut from underneath would be an unlikely and somewhat awkward motion but it can be done. Naturally, the cuts to the 10-2 lines (looking straight at the clock) are the more useful, economical and common. If there is need to go after an angle beyond those, it's generally advisable to use footwork to gain a better angle than to move the blade hand too much.

Also, as you'll notice when practicing, the strikes to the 10-12 line (provided you're in a stance with your knife in your right hand)

are probably easier than strikes to the opposite side (1-2). The situation is reversed when the knife is in your left hand. I've seen exceptions to this, of course. People have different levels of flexibility and coordination. Again, you can overcome any difficulty by footwork and by shifting your upper body to better facilitate the angle.

Stay compact and keep the line so you don't expose yourself like Aaron does in this photo

The Shift

The fencer's shift is similar to the boxer's slip. In doing it, you angle your upper body in order to gain a straight line for your blade to travel so that you don't have to move your arm off the line to hit a target, nor use footwork. (This is, incidentally, a huge problem with quite a few blade systems...they routinely and systematically apply cutting angles that aren't straight, thereby exposing themselves to cuts and grabs.) It is an extremely fast way to take an angle with a strike. In fact, the action is so quick that it's almost imperceptible to all but the most experienced observers.

When you first begin to practice it, you'll be tempted to overdo the shift. The trick is to move only as much as necessary *and* to achieve unity between the shift and the cut. When you can do both simultaneously, you've gained a level of combat efficiency that's hard to overvalue. The shift is so valuable because it allows you to attack an angle with tremendous swiftness, requiring your enemy to be an expert at evasion. As you'll notice when you first begin to shadow fight with your practice blade (never practice with a live blade), footwork and evasion, done right, is an acquired skill even under the best of circumstances. Your enemy in a knife fight, therefore, will likely be at a tremendous disadvantage and be unable to instantly adjust to your cutting angle unless he's practiced too.

The shift will also allow some of those difficult angles – like a 4 cut, for example – with a bit more fluidity than if you were standing upright. And more than this, it carries your head out of the way and helps you be more evasive, which is always a good thing.

Once more, remember that if it's easy to do in training, it'll be quite difficult to apply under pressure. And if it's hard to do in training, it'll never work in a real fight.

The reason for this ought to be obvious, but because of our tendency to think too much about ourselves (all of us are inherently selfish, after all) we forget to take into consideration that the other guy will be moving. When watching a demo of some instructor do his "dance of death" (as Tony Masssengill perfectly puts it) we make a critical error. We stop watching the other guy and focus only on the instructor. Train yourself to avoid this. You'll notice how strange things look when you focus on the other fellow exactly because you'll see how unnatural it is for him to simply freeze for a moment (or longer) in time. That's always the key to everything we're doing. Bruce Lee called those type of demos *"dissecting a corpse"* and so it is. In real life, people don't come forward, throw a strike and then freeze for a moment.

It's in this context that the snap-cut and the shift are seen as the critical elements they are. They can be used on the move (with footwork) and, therefore, avoid leaving you in the danger zone. Simplicity is the key. The more complex the motion, the more likelihood you need to stand your ground – and the more necessary it is for you to have an opponent who stops moving and fighting for some odd reason. In all, if your opponent stops moving and fighting back, you aren't really in a fight – you're in a demo. And this is precisely why the vast majority of knife work (and martial arts too!) is unsuitable for real life – it gets you good at something other than reality.

The Duck & Snap Back

In addition to the shift, which is moving your upper body slightly right or left, you can also move your upper body backwards or forward.

First, you aren't really moving your head forward – you're moving it *down and forward*. This is the duck. If you merely move straight down you're likely to lose your balance so it's better to combine two motions: the squat and the bow, thus eradicating the errors of using either motion solo. A proper duck, therefore, is a motion where you bend forward and move downward in equal fashion simultaneously. As with everything else, only move as much as you need. Don't move too much as that will likely compromise your next movement. And if you bend forward a greater distance than you move downward, you'll break your balance and your shoulders will be facing the floor, thereby breaking your line. The same is true in reverse.

If you need to duck, for whatever reason, the snap-cut can be combined with the movement. By raising the cut, you can still cut an incoming hand or arm or you might cut the leg or groin of the enemy depending upon the situation.

A snap back is when you quickly throw your weight to your back foot. You want to avoid *leaning* back as that will actually slow your footwork down. Leaning back gives you the impression of safety by adding distance but the distance created is artificial. The real distance depends upon your feet and his. The snap-back, therefore, allows you to rapidly move your upper body out of the way and then get right back to your primary position. It should be done with the speed of your snap-cut – dart back, catching the weight in your rear heel, and then shoot forward again. If you have trouble with the snap-back it's usually because your rear leg is too straight. Some people make the mistake of not bending both their knees equally in their ready-position and that mistake will come back to haunt you here because you won't be able to snap-back – you'll only be able to lean, which isn't a motion you want in your arsenal as it's slower than the snap-back and will pin your rear leg down.

Remember, both knees are always bent. To straighten a leg is to compromise your movement speed. To help you understand the difference, imagine that you're standing in a room talking to someone. The conversation grows long (like it would if you were talking to me) and you decide to lean against the wall. When you do this, the weight of your stance is on the wall and your legs are no longer the source of your balance. In this way, a lean and a snap-back can *appear* the same to the untrained eye but they're entirely different as to their actual substance. The proper snap-back uses the legs for speed and snap. The lean moves your upper body back but slows you down by treating your leg like a wall or post rather than as a spring. Another way to see it is that using proper footwork is like paying cash for something; a lean is akin to paying your mortgage with a credit card – you can get away with it here and there, but it's not a good idea.

What to Cut

Jackie's target in this case would be my forward hand.

The obvious answer is whatever you can.

Our full answer, though, is the hands and arms.

In most cases the bad guy will be reaching out to strike and/or grab you. This opens the opportunity for you to cut what targets come forward. If the enemy launches a right-hand punch, angle offline and snap-cut the incoming arm. The force of the cut will be aided by the fact that he's swinging at you. This is why you want a good grip – it should be "loosely secure" as we say. If your grip is too tight you'll slow yourself down and make your hand easier to grab as well as restrict your range. If your grip is weak, though, it can obviously cause a drop.

As for the cut to the arms and hands, people underestimate the effectiveness of simply doing this. They don't think it's that big a deal and assume they need to do something more...well, fancy.

Once more we need to remind you that the context of this book is *self-defense*. We're assuming you have the legal and moral right to use a deadly weapon in your defense. This is especially important. If some dude is taking a swing at you because he thinks you cut him off in line at the Starbucks, and you cut him, you're in more trouble than if you told your wife she looks fat in those jeans.

Also, there's the issue of the follow-up. Quite a few knife demos I see consist of the knife-guru-stud-muffin-master hacking away at the attacker long after the dude's defenseless. We must be certain on this: that's murder, not self-defense. It all looks cool in a video and it might help you impress others who don't know any better, but what you're getting good at is criminality. A way of seeing this is that you have every right to shoot a guy who's breaking into your house, crashing through the front door. But if you chase him down the street pumping lead into him, you've sort of abandoned the whole "imminent" threat thing.

It's the same here. If you use a knife for your defense, you must go out of your way to prove – by your actions – that you weren't trying to kill anyone. You send a strong signal to law enforcement that you were only trying to defend yourself by disengaging as soon as you can.

Quite assuredly, this isn't always the case and we will cover some issues where you need to offer up a more vigorous defense but that's only in the event that you have literally no other choice – such as multiple assailants in your home and you're protecting others and can't flee. But, for the most part, we're going to assume that a serious snap-cut to the arm will render your enemy ineffective.

The force of the cut is increased by the fact that the enemy was bringing their limb into play, swinging it at you. This being the case, the depth of the cut is going to be greater, causing more damage to muscle and tendon. If you catch the enemy on the inside of the arm and/or wrist, his ability to grip is going to be severely compromised. Plus, there will be significant blood loss as well, requiring the assailant to stop doing what he's doing and put some pressure on the wound. This isn't the case in a lot of other cuts and it's precisely why you don't extend your own limb to cut. A cut across the inner arm will degrade anyone's ability to perform athletic functions with their hands, which means, of course, that you've "won" by virtue of removing your enemy's offensive capability.

In every movie you see, if someone takes a knife wound to the arm or leg they can just keep fighting as if nothing happened. This is unrealistic to the point of abject stupidity and, as we've pointed out, leads people to believe that a knife isn't a valid self-defense tool. We should be under no such misapprehensions. Whenever the bad guy reaches out to strike or grab, snap-cut whatever you can. Fingers, hands, wrists and forearms. The inner arm, fingers and hands are extremely vulnerable to the knife and by using good footwork (always using distance control as your best defensive friend) you can continue to snap-cut. Trust me, a heavily bleeding bad guy with a finger cut off is going to have extreme trouble carrying the fight to you. What's he going to grab you with if his fingers and/or hands are cut?

The arms and hands are the perfect target because they're extended toward you, making your counter-offensive strike that much more economical. A thrust to the torso is more dangerous (for you) in that it's slower – having to cover more ground. This is especially pertinent for women, who have less upper body strength than most men, as it makes grabbing them virtually impossible. The very thing they'd grab with, their hands, are what you're attacking. **The great fear of having their knife grabbed and used against them comes from this dual mistake: stabbing instead of snap-cutting and going after the torso rather than the hands/arms.** The JKD knife-fighter who excels at this will have very little opportunity to use escape techniques (which we cover later just in case).

Remember how we talked about the knife being less lethal than the gun? Well, this is the exact manifestation of that advantage. If you fire a bullet, you can't target the guy's hands very well. Because of the stress and speed of a violent encounter, shooters are taught to go for the torso as it's the largest and least mobile target available. A couple of rounds from a handgun are going to cause considerable damage to a bad guy's body, ripping and tearing everything in its path. A knife that cuts the hands and arms is unlikely to have lethal impact even though it demolishes the bad guy's offensive capacity by virtue of taking out his ability to grab, strike or clutch a weapon.

A violent encounter is fluid, though, and no one in their right mind will ever tell you that once you do something or another that the fight is absolutely over. There are always wrinkles in every encounter, peculiar circumstances for which we need to be aware and adapt to, and the great necessity to keep fighting until the threat is fully neutralized or we've escaped.

I simply cannot overstate the necessity, therefore, for you to practice the snap-cut with footwork until it's second nature. By this I mean you literally have to think about the action in order to do it wrong. That's mastery. Many people are content to do something right once or twice. We want to do it right so many times that we have to slow down and think in order to do it wrong! That's excellence – or, as we define it – sustained skill achieved through consistent and focused practice. Good knife fighting skill is simple, but not easy. Move, move, move...and snap cut, snap cut, snap cut. You want speed done right, with small, economical motions impossible to grab because the knife is always in the way. **The snap-cut avoids slashing attacks that leave your weapon off-line – that is, any motion that carries the weapon away from the direct engagement line**. A snap-cut is always a straight motion. Always. Angles are achieved through footwork and upper body movement (the shift). If you try and achieve angles through arm movement alone, you bring the blade off-line, exposing you to the very thing you're trying to do to the bad guy. That's called contradiction. You can get away with mistakes like that here and there but the larger they are, and the more common they are in your execution, the more danger you're putting yourself in. It's like running a red-light. You can get away with it now and then, but you certainly don't want to plan your trip that way.

The next target in terms of efficiency is the face.

I know...I know...this seems almost medieval in its cruelty and appears to contradict what we've been saying about non-lethality. The error is in, however, the misconception of lethality with cruelty. You are fighting, after all. You are working hard to stop the threat. You prefer not to kill anyone and certainly not to do more damage than legally necessary so that you don't end up in prison for the rest of your life. But this doesn't mean you aren't fighting hard! You are seeking the most efficient means of rendering the bad guy incapable of continuing the evil thing he was doing. Cutting his fingers, hands and arms as they extend to you is a very logical way to do this. But what if they're almost on top of you, trying to grab (once more, this is very likely for a woman to encounter) and you can't get at the primary targets without bringing the snap-cut off-line?

The body and face are wide open in such an event.

Of the two, the face is a far better target to snap-cut for the following reasons.

Unlike with a Finger-jab, you don't have to be too
accurate with the knife - just snap-cut his head/face.

First, the face is usually closer. As most people lean forward to
grab and/or strike they bring their face forward. If their face isn't
forward it's because they have extended their hands. It's usually
either/or – a clear case of the limitations of physics and, once more,
why it's essential for us to practice the heck out of the proper snap-
cut and footwork in order to overcome such weaknesses ourselves.
Thus, this target is the application of the principle of striking the
nearest target available. If the arms aren't open, then the face is
exposed. If neither are exposed it's because there is too much
distance. And if there's too much distance, you should be able to run
or get a barrier.

Secondly, a snap-cut to the trunk isn't as effective as one to the
face. To do significant damage to the torso generally requires a larger
blade than we're carrying and/or a stabbing motion. The snap-cut is
designed for hit-and-run tactics, not torso thrusts. It goes back to the
fallacy of the weapon merely being an extension of the hand. That's
nonsense. The weapon changes everything. If you have a hammer,
you don't have a firearm. Or, if you have a rapier, you aren't limited
the way you would be with a small tactical folder.

Know the capacity and limitations of every weapon you have.

A snap-cut to the chest with a tactical folder isn't going to give
you nearly the bang-for-your-buck as a snap-cut to the beak.

Finally, a cut to the face is a horrible trauma for even the most
hardened criminal. It's ghastly to even think about and that's prob-

ably why you recoiled in horror at the thought of it too. I've literally had people tell me they couldn't conceive of "doing that to someone." Well, permit me to be bold. That's a load of stuff I won't mention by name. If you can't differentiate between the morality of self-defense and a rape or murder, you've left the village of reason and moved to la-la land. As personal and horrific as a face cut is, it's sure to be non-lethal and, most importantly, sure to cause the enemy to pause in some way, either due to the damage itself, its psychological impact, and/or because of the blood. Yes, the blood. If you snap-cut the fore-head, he'll bleed so profusely that Rocky after the Apollo Creed fight will look like a male model. And all that blood will make it rather hard to see – and if he has to keep bringing a hand back to wipe blood from his eyes, that's one less hand left with which to attack you with.

As always, we're talking about being able to use the snap-cut in combos of two and three while still moving. I don't care what he's doing – snap-cut and move! Never just stand there. Never. A quick cut to the face can be followed up by another to the hand as you're moving (and he is too...possibly bringing a hand back to his face after the initial attack). As always, don't just stand there and expect one strike to end matters. Move and strike until such a time that:

- You've found an exit
- He's can't or won't attack anymore
- You've got an efficient barrier
- You've fought your way to another weapon like your shotgun
- Police have arrived (at which point you need to drop your knife or get shot)

You'll notice my recommendation to simply snap-cut him in the face. I specifically didn't say to target the eyes or forehead. That's not by accident. Trust me, under pressure you aren't going to be super accurate. Just snap-cut the face and/or head as many times as needed while moving. If you get him in the eye, fine. If you get him in the cheek, fine. Just get him. Snap-cut the target that's easiest to reach. Always. If it's close and in-line, cut it.

Could the cut cause blindness? Of course, but this whole thing wasn't your choice, remember? You are always trying not to be in a fight. This isn't an argument over a parking spot. This is a life-or-death situation where you have logical and legal reason to believe that you'll be killed, raped or gravely injured unless you stop the threat (or those things could happen to someone else such as your spouse or children). Our intent is certainly not to blind the guy but the face is open. To go after another target because we don't want to do that kind of damage implies that this isn't the type of fight for which your knife is required. We've already covered the "don't bring a knife to a gun fight hokum." Well, in all truth, don't bring a knife to a fender-bender fight – that is, a fight where you aren't in such grave danger as to warrant the introduction of a lethal weapon (which a knife is).

CHAPTER 7

FOOTWORK!

ONCE YOU HAVE the basics of the stance, the proper grip and the snap-cut down, it's time to move. We could have started with footwork and then went into the snap-cut but that has the tendency to mix up theoretical principles. You're moving in order to avoid being a target and to take advantage of mistakes by the enemy. Your blade – and the snap-cut – are the very things that "inform" your footwork. In empty hand fighting it's the lead punch. We want to keep the lead hand (and foot) between us and the opponent at all times. It's the same idea here.

Start & finish all footwork in the Ready-Position

An important thing to note is that movement isn't footwork. Foot-work is the scientific transportation of your ready position and your ready position is the stance that best facilitates your snap-cut and supportive footwork. Just moving willy-nilly will more than likely cause disruptions to your ready position, i.e., bring your blade off-line. That being the case, we're going to pay great attention to the integra-tion of these three critical components: the ready position, the snap-cut, and the footwork. *Neither of these three is an end in and of itself but is mutually supportive of and dependent upon the other two.* To understand this is to fully comprehend the big idea of *JKD's Inter-cepting Blade*. To miss the point, however, or to "leave your options open" is to flirt with disaster and repudiate the entire package-deal.

Mistakes can happen. But there's a tremendous difference between making mistakes out of personal error and having one forced upon you because of pressure. Strive for the perfect integration and application of these points in your training. Practice to fluidly achieve consistent, integrated excellence as you move and snap-cut so that if a mistake is made, it's small and infrequent.

The Slide Step

Slide the front foot to the rear to begin the Slide-Step retreat

To do a slide-step, simply slide one foot toward the other and then step with the opposite foot. For example, to go forward, slide the rear foot toward to the front foot, then step with the front. The depth of both the slide and the step need to be the same or else you'll end in a position different than the one you began – thus breaking your on-guard stance.

The finish of the Step-slide retreat

You can gain considerable distance by sliding one foot all the way to the other and then doing the step but you don't always have to do this. You are perfectly free to simply move your sliding foot a few inches, then step with the other foot the same distance. The "small" slide-step is such an efficient means of transportation that it and the next movement, the step-slide, are the primary means of footwork in fighting. This is the case because the proper use of timing and distance is critical to one's success in fighting – with or without a weapon. A small slide-step is so successful in moving your ready-position without disrupting your balance that it's perfect for the demands of real fighting where quick, small adjustments are constantly required.

A full slide-step, where you bring one foot to the other before returning to your on-guard, is the longest type of footwork in your toolbox (covers the most distance).

The Step-Slide

The Step-Slide will cover less ground than the Slide-Step

To move forward in a step-slide, step forward a few inches with the forward foot and then slide the rear foot the equal distance after it. You can do the step-slide in any direction and because of its economical nature, covering ground and changing direction is rather easy once you get the hang of it. For example, you can make two or three rapid step-slides in retreat, then step forward, then over to the right. Or you can step forward, back, back, right, curve left, back again...

You see – it's an excellent transportation tool that allows you unlimited timing and distance control once you're good at it. A good way to practice is to do what's called the footwork square – step forward, then right, then back, then left. This way you'll end up right where you started and it will give your early practice some structure and focus. Once you're good at it, mix in the snap-cut with a practice blade and/or small towel. When you first start to practice, you'll invariably notice that you can do a couple of these rapidly and then you'll want to "shake your legs out." It's normal that tension and fatigue will set in but you must persevere and stay at it. It's absolutely essential that you don't break the conceptual/tactical/technical chain of ready position/snap-cut/footwork. This will take consistent practice and discipline but it's well worth it.

Move the back foot first in the Step-Slide retreat

Because it uses very little room, and most fights are going to be in environments with less than optimal footing, the step-slide is likely to be your most important type of footwork. Naturally, this is a dangerous thing to say due to the vicissitudes of combat, and what you need to do *right now* is always of the utmost importance. Nevertheless, a master of the step-slide is a master of timing and distance, indeed. Perhaps the greatest misconception about JKD and JKD knife fighting is that you need lots of room to use footwork. People will ask me sometimes, *"what if there's no room to move?"* I always answer, "Well, then you're out of luck. But so is your opponent because you've both somehow stumbled into a black hole. Only in a black hole is there no room to move."

Then slide your front foot after it...always careful to
return to the balanced Ready-Position

You see, for the footwork expert there's always room to move. Always. An inch is better than a mile if the inch serves the purpose, so train for inches, not miles. The step-slide will help you achieve this.

Pivot

The pivot is probably the simplest action of all the footwork as it requires only that you swing one foot in a circular direction while the other just has to turn to adjust to the newly created angle. The pivot is usually done off the front leg – meaning that the back leg swings right or left in a circle – but, as always, you can use either leg as the need arises.

As always, we start and finish in the Ready-Position

The pivot may be long or short. Often, during a step-slide or slide-step, it's advisable to add a slight pivot to the navigating foot, thereby creating an angle while moving. Learning to do this – integrating step types – is the key to instantly adjust to the enemy. For example, let's say you are doing a slide-step backwards. As you begin to move your back foot, instead of stepping in a straight line, you can actually pivot instead. Being able to do things like this makes you virtually unlimited in your application abilities. Please note, that whereas the striking actions of your blade appear limited, it's the footwork that keeps the intercepting blade theory from being over-simplistic. True freedom in regard to combat is the ability to out-maneuver your foe and this is achieved only through good footwork. Many people, unaware of this, seek to fill the voids left by their lack of footwork with more and more technique. **This is exactly why complexity is such a danger as it's a sign that the fighter isn't mobile enough.**

To pivot, simply swing the back leg right or left

Balance & Fluidity are always key

Push-Shuffle

A push-shuffle will look just like a step-slide in a still photo because they both follow the same basic rule: move first the foot closest to the direction you're headed. Thus, if you're going forward, the front foot will move first. The thing with the push-shuffle, though, is that if you're going forward the back foot pushes the front. The pushing aspect gives the push-shuffle a more explosive nature than the step-slide. In this way, it's a bit more like a sprint while the step-slide is like a brisk jog. For this reason, the push-shuffle is most often used in direct attacking or defensive motions. To use it for general transportation is superfluous. Many younger fighters, having too much energy, use the push-shuffle like they use the gas-peddle in their car. But just because you can go fast doesn't mean you have to; one should have the discipline to bring the right tool to the job. Like we said, the step-slide and slide-steps are the most used tools of footwork as they allow us to economically cover ground with the least amount of momentum and energy.

The push shuffle should also be used with care due to the fact that its explosiveness could leave us momentarily off balance once the pushed foot lands. Train hard to maintain your balance at all times and endeavor not to overshoot your positional target when using the push-shuffle.

Essential Footwork Drills

There is literally no way to get too good at real footwork. I say *real* footwork because it's the art of moving just enough and at the right time. It's a common error to forget that the footwork is meant to move the on-guard and the on-guard (ready position) is ready to strike with the snap-cut. Footwork, therefore, must be technically sound and trained until you have a reflexive feel to it. One great tip for practice – if you don't have a partner – is the **TV drill**. To do the TV drill, stand in your on-guard stance in front of your TV and every time there's a scene change, you move. This will vastly improve your fighting speed (your timing). A partner can play a better role by suddenly moving at you. The partner should move at different rhythms and depths to force you to instantly adjust the distance. This is called the **mirror drill**.

The stop-cut drill is when your partner steps forward and you instantly snap-cut their hand, arm, or nearest target (always use a hand towel or safe training tool...duh!). This should first be done without the counter-attacker having to use footwork so as to keep the form of the snap-cut from deterioration. Once this is achieved, have the counter-attacker move as they snap-cut too (as needed). As the players get more savvy at the stop-cut, they'll notice they use the shift and other evasive tactics as they counter and move. That's as it should be – just make sure to get back to the on-guard stance.

The *stop-cut drill* should start simple. Once the defender has the mechanics down, they can add evasions to their counter-attack. For example, have the attacker shoot forward and the defender can evade with footwork, then counter with a snap-cut. *All forms of footwork should be practiced separately and then integrated in combinations before the defender attempts to free-flow.* This is the heart-and-soul of the JKD knife method – the counter-attack. Please note that if the defender uses a push-shuffle retreat, he/she can also snap-cut before and during the footwork. If he/she uses a shift, they can cut and shift simultaneously, then pivot and cut, then step-slide back and cut. All of this can be done with great celerity and must be practiced until it's done smoothly.

There are also moments when a stop-cut isn't advisable for some reason. That's okay too. In that event, the knife fighter should move away to reset the distance rather than stand still and admonish themselves for a lost opportunity. Safety is the key thing; if you can't cut immediately, don't worry. But don't stand still. Never, never, never stand still unless you're at a safe distance.

The **circle drill** is a good way to get good at handling fast rushes – especially by another knife-fighter. To do the circle drill, snap-cut and do a series of two, three or even four quick steps *around* the enemy. This action forces the enemy to have to turn in order to get at you and gets you off his line. Many bad guys carry their blade in their rear hand, so this will effectively nullify their charge – especially if you're able to circle to their left (since most people are right-handed). Circular footwork is harder than it looks, so don't despair if you have problems at first. If you have your blade in your right hand and you're stepping to your right, slide the right foot over and then circle the back leg (the left) around. This keeps your blade in-line. It's really a step-pivot you're doing, in fact. The idea is that you're moving around the imaginary circle that forms the safe perimeter that extends out from your enemy.

The ***circle drill*** is absolutely essential to add to your training because it's the perfect answer to the mad rush attack. You simply can't back up faster than your enemy can sprint forward. If that was possible we would have seen somewhere in Olympic history some joker running backwards in a race. For this reason, we must have a highly trained ability to angle – circle really – around an incoming attack without losing our on-guard position. Practice going right and left although, like I said, since most people are right-handed, you'll likely need to move to your right (his left) to best avoid most attacks.

These simple drills should form the basis of your partner training. I don't recommend sparring with your knife (practice knife, of course) because that completely changes the dynamic and we've already covered that. If you want to do that, fine…it's fun. Sure. But it's also contradictory to your basic goals of self-defense and can teach you bad habits and erode your confidence if you have classmates that are better at the sparring than you are. But if you do these drills consistently – and do them until you're able to use them full speed without technical breakdowns – you will have achieved your goal, which is the ability to use your knife against a sudden, violent assault.

CHAPTER 8

TACTICAL VARIABLES AND PROBLEMS

FOR THE MOST PART, a fast combination of snap-cutting supported by quality footwork and the shift, duck or snap-back are more than enough to handle virtually every realistic self-defense scenario. We aren't suggesting that your tactical folder is sufficient to fight off a team of terrorists armed with AK-47's at 100 yards. What we're saying is that JKD style knife fighting is more than sufficient to counter the common threats posed in modern society. But there are a few issues that could complicate your snap-cut-and-move defense. Let's look at them.

If the enemy is somehow able to grab your knife arm you do have a significant problem but all isn't lost yet and you must not panic. By panic I mean stiffen up, stop moving and simply struggle for the knife, muscular force against muscular force. Despite the seriousness of the predicament, the battle is still far from lost. He doesn't have the knife yet! Stay in the fight...don't lose heart. Many women might be tempted to see this scenario as a harbinger of defeat – their worst-case scenario. No. Your worst-case scenario is your death or sexual assault. That hasn't happened yet.

Here are the keys to extricating yourself from grappling scenarios. We'll work the easiest first and move on to more extreme (and risky) escapes as we go.

Footwork & Pull Escape

As always, we want to keep this as simple as possible. Before we do some kind of move, we want to...move! Don't forget to keep moving. If you can, keep moving and use the power of your footwork, combined with pulling your blade back to your body (think of pulling your elbow back to your hip...don't focus on your wrist). This is the easiest of all the escapes and the least risky. If you're moving and snap-cutting it's going to be quite difficult for your enemy to get a good grip on an initial grab. The mistake you want to avoid is freezing once there's contact, which would allow him to gain ground and secure his grip – probably by bringing in both hands. If you stay mobile and pull the blade toward your hip, thus lowering it from the line, you'll make it extremely hard for anyone to maintain their grip. This is especially true for women when fighting a larger, taller man. By pulling the blade back toward their hip, the enemy will be forced to bend over, which will neutralize his advantage in upper body strength.

Practice this with a partner and get used to the action. As always, staying relaxed and mobile – using explosive speed with as little muscular tension as possible – takes practice.

We should note that the general *snap-cut and move* defense has in mind an attacker that's rushing forward to grab, so this first scenario –where you're grabbed – is an extension of our primary tactical mindset. We are expecting the bad-guy to try and grab us.

The footwork and pull defense is, therefore, merely a rational corollary of our primary knife-fighting tactic.

When doing the pull, you may be able to turn the blade so that it cuts the hand or arm that's grabbing you. You should absolutely do this if possible. Sometimes the attacker has a position that leaves you incapable of doing this safely (usually for the security of your grip). In that event, no worries. Just use your footwork and pull the blade back toward your hip.

If you don't succeed at first, you can always try again. Keep moving – maybe change directions. The second or third time might be a charm. The **fake-stab**, which we'll cover at the end of this section, will come in very handy in such a case.

Once again, though, if you're moving and snap-cutting, and you don't bring the blade high (off-line) where your wrist is exposed, the chances of the enemy getting a significant grip is quite remote. The execution of proper fundamentals will make grappling scenarios as likely as finding a happy Hillary voter the day after Trump won.

The Drop-Shift & Pull

A more extreme scenario might call for a *drop-shift* to be used with the pulling action. A drop-shift is a bit like a boxer's ducking motion. The point of this action is to suddenly bend your knees and hips so violently (thus lowering your center of gravity *and pulling the knife away),* that the enemy loses his grip. He may have been prepared for you to go backwards, right or left – but not downward. You must be careful that you don't go down too fast and thereby lose your balance and/or bring the attacker down on top of you. The depth of the drop-shift is calibrated to the necessity of your freeing action. Only move as much as you need to and no more.

The Step-through Drop & Pull

A variation of this is the *step-through drop-shift*. To do this success-fully, you need to actually change leads as you drop your hips down and pull your blade back. Thus, if you have your right forward, pull your right side completely to the rear – not forgetting to violently pull the right elbow back simultaneously – as you drop into your crouch. This is sometimes called the "pivot escape" too since there's a pivoting action to your footwork. Either way will work – straight back with the step-through or pivoting slightly right or left depending upon which side you had forward. They're basically the same action in spirit and all three things – the step-through, the drop, and the pulling of the knife arm – must be done simultaneously for the best results. As always, you want to practice this against a partner to get a feel for it but if that's not possible – if you live on an island and/or no one likes you – make sure to practice in the air. Making these "escapes" a part of your shadow fighting drills will greatly enhance your fluidity and, more than that, help you overcome the fear of being grabbed in the first place.

The Fake Stab

Lastly, the *fake stab* is absolutely essential to your success in such actions. If your knife hand is grabbed, press forward suddenly like you're going for a stab and then shoot backward with your escaping/freeing action. The *fake stab* will force the enemy to push you away or else he'll get stabbed. At that point, reverse directions and do the *footwork and pull* or one of the others. This simple maneuver will allow you to overcome great deficits of strength and should almost always precede one of the escaping actions if the enemy has a good grip on you. The false stabbing motion can, in fact, actually stab the bad guy in the stomach if he's not quick to react, so don't be half-hearted with the action. Practice this diligently so that the actions can be performed in seamless combination and you'll be virtually impossible to disarm.

The Slash, the Stab & the Saw

In the event that you're overpowered and grabbed in such a fashion that footwork is impossible (you're on the ground, pinned against a wall, etc.), more extreme measures are necessary.

If you're pinned down and your knife is free, use it to slash or stab whatever target is available. (Remember: we aren't against slashes and stabs; we just use them appropriately). The best targets are the inside of the leg (femoral artery) and neck or throat for slashes. The slash should be hard and deep. The blood loss from either of these motions will be severe and the enemy will have very little time left for his assault. Obviously, these actions are likely to prove deadly. That isn't a violation of our previous points. It's simply a terrible consequence of the enemy putting us in a position where the other options are unworkable.

If the enemy has you by the hair/head or around the waist, for example, footwork and snap-cuts are hard to achieve. Also, it's important to know that you probably want to avoid trying to slash or snap-cut a hand due to the proximity, which could lead you to cutting yourself in the process. By all means, though, if you can simply cut the inside of the guy's arm instead of slashing the throat, do that! But we're talking about an absolutely worst-case scenario where there are no other options.

To do a proper slash, remember to keep the action small. Use the elbow to drive and direct the power and angle of the cut. If you focus on the knife itself there's a tendency to become too wild in the motion. As with the snap-cut, speed is essential – and so is frequency.

Cut hard and often. If you hesitate because you fear killing someone you very well may be killed because of your hesitance. We've already considered the realities of a knife fight – morally and legally. This isn't a time for obfuscation. You must slash and keep slashing until the enemy has let you go.

The stab works quite well against the abdomen. Depending upon the blade you're carrying, though, pretty much any target is vulnerable. The issue is that if you don't have a guard protecting your hand, and the shock of the action causes your hand to slip, you very well might cut off your own fingers. Knife wounds to the hand are one of the first things to look for when seeking the perpetrator of a knife attack. Remember O.J. Simpson after the murders of Nicole Simpson and Ronald Goldman? He had several wounds on his hands. That's pretty good evidence he had stabbed someone and the knife had slipped. He told police (if memory serves) that he'd cut his hands while making a sandwich. Well, I don't know about you but if I cut myself more than once while preparing a snack I'd probably just give up. I mean, how many wounds are too many for a peanut butter and jelly? Just order a pizza at that point and get some bandages.

Anyway, as with the other actions, make sure you move fast, stay accurate and keep at it until you break free. This is a deadly situation and you must not lose – you cannot lose. You must be as calm as you can under the circumstances and yet fierce too.

Please understand that we aren't trying to kill anyone. These tactics are exactly what we're fighting to avoid with the footwork and snap-cut – with the *way of the intercepting/stopping blade*. But violence being violence, we sometimes have to do more than we want. We already have to do more than we want just by having the knife in our hands.

The last action is called the "saw" because it's a situation where you're actually using the blade in a sawing action against the enemy's arm. This comes into play when they have you and your blade arm locked up. What you do is turn the blade toward whatever skin you can find and drive it in a kind of sawing action. If you can bring your other hand around for help, place it on the back of your blade for added power and drive the weapon into the enemy's flesh or bone. Of course, your free hand can also be used for attacking too – you can punch and eye-jab as well – but if you can use it to help secure your weapon and facilitate the saw, do that instead. Cutting is generally always better than punching and poking.

A variation of the saw is the scoop. The scoop is like using the knife as you would an ice-cream scooper. Just like that. You get the idea.

The Hand-off and Stalemate

A final issue you can consider is the **hand-off** – that is, you change hands, pass the knife from one to the other. Now, obviously, this is wrought with danger in the event that you drop the weapon or it's intercepted by the enemy. This should only be done in the most extreme circumstance when the other options have all failed. The key to the handoff is to make it as close a maneuver as you can – don't toss it from hand to hand but literally bring the other hand in, place it on top of the knife hand, and change possession. This will limit the chances of a drop. Again, a proper handoff is done by covering the one hand with the other and changing possession. It's never advisable to let go of your knife without the other hand already having a grip.

Like everything here, practice is needed to achieve this. It's simple, yes – but not easy.

We pause once more to reiterate how dangerous a scenario we're talking about – and how rare. If you're moving and snap-cutting, the chances of someone getting a solid grip on you are slim. Thus, what we're discussing should be seen as extraordinarily rare and dangerously stupid. Possibly, the only thing more dangerous is voicing a political opinion on Facebook. Changing grips or hands in the middle of a fight is no small matter as there are numerous ways to lose your weapon. And getting stabbed by your own knife has got to be pretty high on the list of things you don't want to happen.

Therefore, if all else fails – and there's no safe way to either transfer the weapon to the other hand or free it, choose a **stalemate**. Yes, as long as the weapon is stalemated and you still have it, so long as there isn't another threat imminent, you still have your safety. Not only that, you still have the opportunity to escape here and there if the bad guy loses focus. Unless you're in the wilderness fighting off zombies after civilization collapses, there's generally a time-limit on the enemy's efforts. And even in that case, there's still a chance Rick Grimes might find you before the zombies eat your face. By making enough noise and taking enough time, the bad guy will generally have to take his show on the road. After all, your enemy's goal was your death or injury or rape, right? Well, he can't do any of that and still hold onto you while you hold onto your blade. That's a win.

Think about that.

Never, never, never give up that knife.

Learn to lock it down if you have to. Use your other hand to secure it and keep it from being pulled from your grasp. With a little practice, you'll be surprised how hard it is to unlock a blade from your grip. Often times, in fact, you see videos of police – several of them – struggling to put cuffs on an unwilling criminal. A lot of people see something like that and they're puzzled. They think, "hey, what's going on with the police? Why are they having trouble subduing that dude? Aren't they highly trained specialists? Don't they have some kind of technique to get someone to instantly comply with their legal wishes?"

Yes, they do. It's called a bullet.

You see, it's not very easy to put cuffs on someone that refuses to comply. A non-cooperative person who fights like a cat trying to stave off a bath is almost impossible to control without some help. That's just the way it is. We are conditioned by too many movies and stupid demos where the alleged master can do virtually anything to anyone. But the reality is far different. Incidentally, I think this misconception is at the heart of much of the bad publicity the police have received in the past few years. You have people who have never been in a fight in their lives watching a video of police wailing on someone and they think it's all too much. They think a cop should know some move or another without having to *really* hurt anyone. That's a bunch of nonsense. But it's nonsense that we need to be aware of because if we're ever forced to fight for our own blade, we must remember that *it's us who have the advantage.* In such a struggle, bring the knife lower, keep your grip, use both hands if you have to and don't let go. Keep trying to move too, and punch the dude with your free hand if you can do so – a stalemate might open up an opportunity to start moving again. But no matter what – don't give up! Fight!

You're stronger than you think. Even in this horrible scenario, don't give up. Just because you can't use the weapon directly doesn't mean it's not still of use.

More Extreme Scenarios – they have a gun, or a knife!

Please understand the gravity of the situations we're about to discuss. Your enemy has a gun or a knife. The slightest mistake can kill or seriously injure either you or someone else. We aren't talking about a demo at the school or some kind of nonsense like that. I sometimes see an instructor demonstrate a defense against multiple armed attackers. You probably have too. People who think they can disarm several violent men are in the same league as people who think they can fly after watching a Superman movie.

Here are our basic rules in such events.

Run!!!

I know, I know...you can't always run away, but if you can, get going. This should be your general reaction to all violent things, frankly, but it's especially pertinent now.

If you get into a struggle for a weapon you have to be at close range, which makes any mistake insanely dangerous. It's easier to shoot or stab you, after all, if you're right in front of me instead of running and ducking. This sounds like an easy enough point – rather obvious, in fact – but I'm always surprised by how under stress we can lose focus on the basics. Most people aren't very accurate with their guns in the first place, so standing still like you're a paper target when you know they're going to shoot is only helping the shooter. Start running and dodging. Run around things, between things and so on. Maybe he misses. Or, maybe he hits you but doctors can fix the damage. I know that sucks and I wish I could tell you otherwise, but you must face the facts. Running away and refusing to stand your ground is always the best approach to "fighting" an assailant with a knife or gun.

You will rarely ever see someone running down the road trying to shoot or stab someone. It's hard to do and it heightens the bad guy's chance of being apprehended by the police. So, before you start worrying about a bunch of moves that will probably not work, move...run...avoid.

Intercept

If a bad guy is reaching into his pocket or waistband it usually isn't to give you flowers or cash. He's probably going for a weapon. Just like police officers are trained to watch people's hands, you should too. As they say, the eyes are the windows to the soul but the hands to his intent. Watch the hands!

We can't possibly cover every contingency here but the basics are for you to immediately grab his wrist as he reaches for his weapon. With your free hand, bring your knife into play. Whether you instantly use it, or merely threaten him so that he'll comply is dependent upon many factors. The principle is that you must have justification for your action – you must have reasonable suspicion he was going for a weapon.

If they threaten you with the weapon (and you don't have your weapon deployed)

Comply with their demands unless you're sure that in doing so you or your loved one will be killed or raped.

The reality of this situation is that the bad guy has the drop on you. They have their weapon in play already. If it's a gun, and they wanted you dead, they would have already started shooting. If they haven't started firing already, though, it's because they want something – usually money. Just give it to them. Seriously. It's stupid to gamble that you can beat him. And that's what you're doing – you're betting that your skills at beating a guy with a gun or knife in a live scenario is worth the $100 bucks you have in your pocket.

Imagine this: if a buddy wanted to bet you that you could stop him from shooting you in the face, would you do it? Not with a live gun! That's just nuts. And that would be a bet where you might win money from your knucklehead friend. In this case, you don't have anything to win except the money you already have. That's crazy.

The proper way to see this, therefore, is to be vigilant about your personal safety – prevention is always better than cure. Avoid high risk environments and never, never carry something with you that you aren't willing to part with unless you take even more extreme measures of precaution. For example, let's say that you have to drive a bunch of cash to the bank for some reason. Maybe your grandmother is getting senile and she gave you five big ones in your birthday card this year. I don't know...but you have to take it to the bank, or go bury it in your back yard. Whatever. The thing to do is to make sure you go to the bank when it's open. Don't stand there at the ATM at midnight. If you had to do something like that for some crazy reason, and you don't have friends you can trust (to bring them with you for extra security), call the police and ask for an escort. Tell them you tried to go to the bank and you thought you saw some suspicious activity.

The point is that you want to be ahead of the game, not reacting.

So much of these "guy has a gun to your face" scenarios are bewildering in the extreme because you have to ask yourself how they happened in the first place. Never forget this: *if you spend a little time in making sure you aren't doing stupid stuff, you won't have to spend lots of time practicing how to extricate yourself from the consequences of doing that stupid stuff.*

If you're strolling downtown with your wife, going out to dinner and stuff like that, by basically staying in the main shopping areas, you should be fine. Bad guys usually don't walk down main street at 8pm and rob people at gunpoint. If you live in such a place where that happens and you can't move someplace safer, just make sure you don't carry your life's savings with you at any single moment, and try to place physical barriers between you and would-be criminals. All of that beats trying to fight a guy who has the drop on you with a weapon.

In all, a lot of trouble can be avoided if you aren't stupid. I don't say this to be flippant. I'm serious. If you're out drinking at 2am and you're carrying credit cards and loads of cash, you simply aren't very bright. Being inebriated in public is always a bad idea – always. First, you better not be driving! Second, your reflexes are slower. Third, your situational awareness and judgment are greatly diminished. No one ever tells a story that starts, *"Dude, the most awesome thing happened to me. I was absolutely drunk the other day..."*

I know it's politically incorrect to say these days but for the sake of truth I must point it out. You are never *absolutely safe*. No one is. The key to success in combat is to know yourself and your enemy – truly, not lying to yourself and not avoiding unpleasant facts. If you have something that someone wants, you must ask yourself what it is, who wants it, and under what circumstances the aggressor might confront you. That's what situational awareness is. Another way to see it is to ask yourself, what might motivate my enemy? A few years ago, there was a terrible case where a college student was found having sex in public with a young woman who had passed out. As it went, a few people spotted them in the dark behind a dumpster. How romantic. Well, during the legal proceedings it was reported that the couple had been at a bar drinking all night. So, we have two young college students, with hormones raging, dancing and all that, drunk out of their minds, and having the time of their life. She left with him willingly. On the way to wherever they were going, she passed out.

The legal situation got all the press because the rapist was given a light sentence. Feminists howled in protest at the leniency. Our point is that every young woman should know that there are unscrupulous men out there who would welcome the opportunity to give them alcohol (or worse!) in order to lower their defenses. In this case, the "enemy" is the sexually charged male who wants sex. Situational awareness would demand that every woman who is concerned with her safety recognize this and never accepts a drink from others (that might be drugged) or allows herself to drink in public to the point where she can't think straight. No woman should ever violate this rule. You can gripe all you want that there shouldn't be men that sexually abuse women. You're certainly welcome to do that but it's very much like screaming at the sky to stop raining.

A prime example of this point is Bill Cosby. How many women accepted drinks from him that were drugged? No woman should accept a drink from a man in such instances, nor should they get drunk in public. Know your enemy!

Because of political correctness, though, voicing such obvious facts runs the risk of getting you accused of "victim blaming." That's utter cow stuff too. It's the presumption of absolute safety, devoid of personal responsibility, that is wrong and you must reject it whole-sale. Like I said earlier, once you're in a fight, the person's politics are irrelevant. The same thing goes here too. Always ask what motivates your enemy, where your enemy could be found, and adjust accordingly.

Personally, I have never been in a bar (except to pick up a friend once or twice) or any place where there are likely to be inebriated men. I am perfectly free to do so and I'd love to live in a world where I don't have to worry about drunken buffoons getting aggressive because they say I bumped into them on the way to the bathroom. But all of that is nonsense. What matters is the reality of the situation. And the reality is that no environment where there are copious amounts of drugs and/or alcohol is safe.

Let me give you another quick example.

A friend of mine had a violent incident a few years back. They had an adult sibling that had all sorts of drug problems and they let her stay at the house with them for a few weeks. It was their sister, they said, and they "had to be there for them." Okay. Fine. The problem is, this friend also had children too and their first responsi-bility is to the safety of their home. Well, apparently, the sister, told a few male friends where she was staying and bragged about how wealthy her sibling was. That, obviously, got the attention of the men who inquired about the usual: cash, jewelry and electronics (what... you thought I'd say classic literature and cheese?). You know, the same thing everyone asks about their neighbors, right?

So, you can see where this is going. They broke in one day when they figured everyone would be at work and school. The problem is, the teenage daughter was home sick when they kicked the backdoor in. My friend had a big dog that barked a lot but the drug addled sister had informed her fine friends that the dog was just a barker, not a biter. Sure enough, he barked but then actually ran outside and played in the yard while they ransacked the house. The daughter was, thankfully, unharmed but badly shaken up. Things could have been tragically worse that day and, as is often the case, it could have all been avoided if my friend had thought things through and tried to help his sister in a way that wouldn't put his family in the crosshairs of people who might want his stuff.

All said, if you live a relatively logical lifestyle your chances of having a weapon pulled on you are quite remote. And then, even if you win the unlucky lottery and find yourself at the business end of a barrel, it's probably because the gun holder wants money. In that event, be smart and hand over the money/credit card/phone. To fight for them isn't worth the risk.

They have a weapon & you must fight

There are other instances where you truly, truly win the unlucky lottery and come face-to-face with a deranged person or persons hell-bent on evil. This could be a case of an active shooter or terrorist or rapist. The point here is that logic tells you compliance isn't going to save you. The thing to remember, therefore, is that you're starting from a premise that you're going to die and/or be raped if you do nothing. My thought is, no one should ever go down without a fight. Cowering and pleading with a terrorist for your life as he coldly walks around shooting people is not something anyone reading this book should consider as a good option. I cannot stress this enough – going down without a fight is a shameful thing. Moreover, there is absolutely no excuse for an adult male giving up and cowering when he knows he'll be killed. There is no honor in refusing to fight if escape, concealment and resistance are futile. No matter the horror of the encounter and no matter how set in stone your demise may look, you must not give up.

Fight!

Again, this is politically incorrect these days but the truth is that it is your responsibility to defend yourself. The police cannot be everywhere. The right to self-defense is yours alone and even if you are the worst fighter in the world, it's still an honorable thing to fight back vigorously – with all your love and all your hatred of evil – when facing death. This point alone shows the appalling evil of "gun-free" zones across the West. The denial of one's right to defend themselves with a weapon is a human rights violation of epic proportions. In the face of evil, if you've been *legally* (but immorally) disarmed, you have been made the victim twice.

The difference between the Holocaust and a Civil War is whether the population is armed to defend itself. And the difference between you being in the fight or not is whether you have a weapon. The moral principle is simple enough for even children to understand. A slave cannot legally defend himself and anyone or any government that takes away your right to defend yourself makes you their slave too.

When you understand this, you'll have the proper mentality – and proper attitude is essential to survival in a fight. Technique follows attitude and strategy. Never forget that.

When fighting a person with a weapon your footwork and movement are paramount. Against a gun, angle more to stay offline and try to cut the hands. You need to be as evasive as you can. Your knife isn't going to block bullets or another knife. As we've already covered, move! But beyond that, the good news is that the principles of combat are the same: cut their hands and arms. You may have to use cunning and deception; you may have to use concealment against a deranged gunman. Use whatever you have to but certainly fight. This is a question you must settle beforehand, though. You must understand that you won't likely survive certain types of fights – and multiple shooters with AK-47's would be one of them. Your tactical folder (assuming that's all you're carrying) against that type of firepower is a pretty grim scenario.

But, you know what? Who cares! Maybe you can conceal yourself and then take one of the shooters out. Cut the arm, grab the weapon and keep cutting. Repeat. Now you have their gun.

Listen, I'm not going to promise you anything. But if you die in that kind of fight, so be it. At least you fought. And at least you were diligent enough to have had a weapon with you. Imagine if most of the citizens of our nation did the same thing. That would certainly change the dynamic of the active shooter issues we currently face today. Many people say there's nothing you can do in a situation like that. Nonsense. That's a dangerous thing to believe. There's always something you can do right up until the moment when you're dead. When you're dead you can't do anything. Until that time, however, you should be thinking, planning, moving, and taking any smart action you can. To simply wait to die without trying to fight and/or escape isn't an action worthy of someone who loves life. And to love – truly love – you must also abhor evil and that abhorrence can fuel you to take action. Take it! Even if you die. Dying isn't the worst thing that can happen to a person. Living a life of cowardice and dishonor is.

Active shooter incidents happen in gun-free zones; they happen in places where the attacker knows his targets are unarmed. Well, imagine a world where 10 or 15 people are carrying knives. Imagine that some shooter goes into a place and starts firing and instead of running for cover, a dozen people swarm him – knives drawn.

Imagine that they carve him up and he bleeds out slowly, in great agony. That would stop these ridiculous scenarios right then and there. The next potential mass-murderer is going to hear about that and think to himself, *"Well, I certainly don't want to get stabbed to death by a throng of angry defenders. That would suck."*

A mass-shooter is simply a bully with a gun. If he thinks he's going to take serious blowback from his aggression, he'll simply move on. If you find this hard to swallow I ask you to look at the lessons of history. Weakness always invites aggression, so if you truly want to limit aggression and violence, encourage strength, not weakness.

On the other hand, there are those out there who expect me to give them some super effective technique that will allow them to handle multiple gunman or something like that. Sorry. Everything we covered is still the same. You can change some of the targets (like adding the throat instead of the face) but that's it. Apply the basics and cut the arms/hands. Keep it simple. But you have to think and move too. Keeping a clear mind under stress is incredibly important. You must not give in to panic even though you're freaking out. And if you're always assuming that someone else is going to keep you safe, then trust me, you'll panic.

In all, please, please remember, keep it simple and simply fight. I'm sure someone can always look back, after the battle, and tell us how the perfect plan would have done such and such. The problem is that in sudden violent scenarios, like the ones we're discussing, there is no way to plan because there are too many variables. Patton once remarked that a violent and swift plan executed today beats the perfect one next week. I think that's the truth here. Take these principles, tactics and techniques – have the right attitude – and fight if there are no other options. That decision is yours and yours alone. In making it, you become much stronger simply by virtue of having an attitude of realism.

CHAPTER 9

A FINAL WORD

THERE ARE many other things I could say about this subject. But to do that would violate the primary objective of the book, which is to give you, the reader, a simple and direct knife method. I do sincerely hope that you're aware of the danger of complexity. We live in a day of tremendous technological advancement. I'm writing this on a laptop that was inconceivable to me just 20 years ago. But though there have been profound technological improvements throughout our life, these achievements have not altered the nature of human violence and ethics. No. There may be a heightened level of complexity in our computers, but fighting with a knife is still a fast moving crisis where major decisions on strategy and motor reflexes must have been taken care of beforehand.

In all, a great many of us wander into our lives, growing older, accumulating things left and right, and end up wondering how things got so busy. It's complexity-creep; it's the mistaken notion that more will always be better. But we know that money won't buy us happiness and a loving family with enough is better than a contentious, broken one with opulence. Nevertheless, it's hard not to keep going into debt – to look at things and say, *"can I afford the monthly payment?"* rather than, *"do I need this?"* It's exactly this that's at the heart of Bruce Lee's JKD and it's what I'd like to leave you with as a parting thought.

I once asked Ted Wong why it was so hard to get JKD to the average person. In short, I asked him why JKD wasn't more popular. He didn't hesitate with an answer. People don't understand and respect simplicity, he said. This leads instructors to offer more and more stuff, regardless of whether or not the extra stuff detracts from our ability to function in reality or not. Well, this was precisely the burden of this book. I offer you what amounts to one cutting action – the snap-cut – and the attending on-guard position and footwork. Along with this I've provided just a few simple drills too. But please don't misunderstand this and think it's not enough or somehow insufficient. That would be a colossal mistake.

Consider the fistic prowess of Mike Tyson. In his prime, Mr. Tyson may very well have been the ultimate hand-to-hand fighting machine. Personally, I have never seen anything remotely close to his capability when he was in his heyday. And what did he do to attain this? He jogged. He worked the bags, shadow-boxed, and worked the focus mitts. And he sparred and studied boxing tactics. That's it. There were no fancy secrets to his workouts. In fact, he focused *more* on the basics than other people. If there was a secret, that was it. Every boxer knows not to walk straight in and fire shots. Tyson took this seriously and was constantly working on evasive head-movement – so much so that he became a fearsome *defensive* wizard. He was impossible to hit clean and often. Because of all that head-movement and that defensive skill, he was able to viciously counter-attack when guys missed him. Indeed, early Tyson once called himself an aggressive counter-puncher. That's right! He was renowned for his offensive ferocity but, in reality, he was aggressively defensive. Jack Dempsey, who Tyson modeled himself after incidentally, considered himself to be a master of *aggressive defense.*

That's what you've got here too. You've got an aggressive counter-attack methodology with a knife. Instead of looking for another ten thousand things to do with the blade, master this. Don't fall into the trap of being mediocre with lots of stuff. Instead, go all-out in the pursuit of simple mastery. If your footwork, timing and snap-cut are first-rate you can all but guarantee that you'll be safe in anything but the most extreme environment – such as you get attacked by a SEAL team or something.

I'm certainly not saying that no other knife method will work. Please don't misconstrue all this. I'm not saying that any more than I'm asserting you should abandon firearms in lieu of tactical folders. It's just that JKD's way of the blade is built upon consistent and non-contradictory principles that mesh perfectly with the reality of moral and legal self-defense. Its simplicity shouldn't ever be looked at as a limitation but as the summation of correct balance between theory and practice. Every movement is ruthlessly vetted to make sure there are no "extras" and JKD, both its empty hand and knife methods, is virtually alone in this regard. So, when you see the complexity of other approaches, train your eye to see the danger of the movements. Train your eye to see the impossibility of the enemy simply standing there and waiting. And notice how the many so-called "advanced" knife movements are actually just dangerously excessive angles that expose you, the self-defender, to even more danger since your blade is off-line.

JKD's blade method is comprehensive according to its own princi-ples. It isn't Kali. It isn't all things. If it's everything, then it's nothing. All things are specifically what they are and aren't something else in the same context (law of identity and law of non-contradiction). We need to keep that in mind.

As we've covered, the tactical folder is not a knife we'd prefer to fight with – it's the one that we're forced to fight with in modern life. We note that most Kali fighters in antiquity were using longer blades themselves, more akin to the machete, in their war arts. This treatment is, therefore, an attempt to be consistent with the demands of modern self-defense, both legally and tactically. The lack of offensive capacity for killing with the tactical folder (when compared to longer blades like machetes and swords) is not actually a contradiction or weakness in the JKD method when seen in this light. After all, the more offensive knife tactics, as opposed to JKD's counter-offensive approach, are the ones that will run afoul of modern legality due to their violation of self-defense fundamentals.

Beyond that, JKD's knife fighting method has no fundamental weaknesses or drawbacks. What it purports to do, it does. Obviously, there is always the issue of user error – that is to say, the practitioner himself may fail to perform under pressure. This is why proper attitude (without which awareness becomes impossible) and consistent training are so important. JKD's blade method isn't perfect if by that you mean a panacea; we are merely asserting that it is a proper and non-contradictory method for small blade use for the purpose of self-defense in modern life. There is no such thing as perfection here under the sun. Perfection resides in the being of God, not in any man-made system and certainly not in any application. This is another error I hope to help you avoid. I sometimes hear people in martial arts speak of "pure" this and that...you know, *pure Wing Chun or pure JKD*. That's all a bunch of malarkey. We're talking about fighting systems. That's all. Our combat preferences – regardless of what they're called...BJJ, Muay Thai, Glock, Mossberg, whatever – are simply tools.

Reality is pure. Our methods, in that light, are merely our meager attempts to adapt to the reality that's always challenging us because, simply put, none of us has ever had, or ever will have, comprehensive knowledge. We can have true knowledge – that which isn't contradictory and accurately conforms to the facts of reality – but never comprehensive knowledge. We know as a man knows, which is in finitude, and never as God knows. Much confusion about martial art can be eradicated if we all understood this point.

So, for me to say that JKD's way of the blade is what it is and it's not something else is not to claim that it's a *pure or perfect* methodology of knife fighting. On the contrary, this is said in the service of proper identification. If we start bickering about which method is pure or something like that, we've flipped the equation and have put the burden on training rather than on conforming to reality. But our goal should never be achieving fidelity to a system at the expense of realism. Doing so, of course, is problematic because reality must take precedence over the system designed to conform to it. This is the weakness in all tradition – it replaces the conformity to reality (truth) with adherence to man-made rules.

With that said, let us finish with this statement: if these principles of knife fighting which we have called JKD's *way of the intercepting blade* conform to the reality of modern self-defense, then let us use them. If they don't or, quite importantly, if the real-world demands change suddenly and we find ourselves in a new kind of reality, then let us forget them. The issue before us now and always is *what is the truth?* This is why I've said that all of us are philosophers – especially those of us that take up arms to defend ourselves.

As it stands now, given the current conditions of history, I offer you this brilliant method. Its brilliance is in its unique capacity to accurately conform to the demands of real-world self-defense – morally, legally and technically. It's the method for the modern self-defender and it shouldn't worry us in the least that we aren't training to be more offensive with the tactical folder. Nothing should jolt us from the security of the proper moral reasoning of self-defense. This is the simple genius behind JKD's way of the blade. It's simply, in my opinion, a nearly flawless self-protection method to be used in extreme scenarios because of its coherence to the facts of reality. Being so direct and simple, it doesn't break down under combat stress as other methods are prone to do. Being heavily reliant upon footwork and avoidance, it keeps the student from spending long, hard hours of practice perfecting a technique that might never occur in a real fight. And, more still, by practicing the art of not being there (footwork) the student will have an answer for things they couldn't possibly have trained for in advance due to the fact that no bad guy can do the physically impossible: he can't hurt what he can't reach.

Furthermore, JKD's insistence upon counter-attack keeps you safe both physically and legally. The counter-attack is the safest means of attack. By exploiting the enemy's offensive stroke, the defender is able to greatly limit their own exposure to danger. In a way of seeing it, the counter-fighter is the true self-defender, taking advantage of the very thing they won't themselves do – that is, attack another human being. This is the heart of the JKD *intercepting* philosophy.

And lastly, when all is said and done, JKD's way of the blade is the correct moral balance between a skillful, vigorous defense and immoral, illegal assault.

It's my fervent hope and prayer that you, the reader, never in a million years need to use the material presented. But if you do, it's even more my prayer that you are a moral warrior – that you fight with honor, skill and love. As I said previously, self-defense, the action, is a profoundly moral thing. I like to think that there is an inherent beauty in this knife fighting method – a deadly beauty, yes, but a beauty indeed. And I like to think this is so because of these aforementioned facts.

May God bless you and your training and may good people never have anything to fear from you as you learn to defend yourself and loved ones.

Printed in Great Britain
by Amazon